BOOTS, BALLS AND HAIRCUTS

An Illustrated History of Football from Then to Now

Hunter Davies

First published in Great Britain in 2003 by Cassell Illustrated,
a division of Octopus Publishing Group Limited
2-4 Heron Quays, London E14 4JP

A CIP catalogue record for this book is available from the British Library.

Editor: Victoria Alers-Hankey
Designer: Austin Taylor

ISBN 1 84403 0326

Printed in China

CONTENTS

INTRODUCTION:

Going to the Match

I WENT TO A MATCH TODAY. It was Spurs at home against Leeds
United, not that that matters too much in the scheme of things, as they
have played each other many times, nor the score. The date was
November 24, 2002, which does matter, marginally, because I'm trying
to get down on paper the personal experience and observations of going
to a match at this particular time in our particular football history.

It was a Sunday, which was annoying. I always think nature intended
football matches to be on Saturday afternoons. That's how I was brought
up, how all supporters were brought up, since league games began.
It's only recently, in the last ten years, they've started mucking about
with the fixture list. Today a game can be on almost any day, at almost
any time.

It was a Premiership game, which was what the top division in
England was called, at that time, in that season of our Lord, 2002–3.
Leeds that day were managed by Terry Venables, formerly of Spurs,
both as a player and manager, so that gave some extra interest. He had
taken over at Leeds a few months earlier, but was not doing well.

I have memories of Leeds playing at White Hart Lane in the 1970s,
under Don Revie, and can recall the quality of their skill and passing, a
team playing as a total unit. Can't remember which game, or the score.
I must have seen almost a thousand games by now, but as each one gets
replaced by the next, the facts of the old one fade. The body
movements, the emotions, the faces, they remain. I can still see Jimmy
Greaves hanging around the penalty area, Dave Mackay with his chest
out, Hoddle's too-short shorts, Gazza's head shaking ever so slightly,

Klinsmann diving, arms out, Ginola standing, arms on hips, Robbie Keane buzzing like a clockwork toy. Which he was today, so obviously I can still see him clearly.

I decided to follow Spurs in 1960 when we came to London. It doesn't normally happen like that. Supporters inherit a team through their family, or where they live, but I'd left my hometown, which is Carlisle, and wanted a London club to follow. Arsenal and Spurs were roughly equidistant from our house, but Spurs, at that moment, were more exciting. I can never abandon them, but I have also, over the years, gone to watch Arsenal, which my son thinks is disgraceful, totally disloyal, how could I. My explanation is that I follow football first, wanting to see a good game, and secondly I want to see Tottenham win.

I used to stand on the Shelf, on the terraces, then I sat for a few years at the Paxton Road end with my son when we were both Members, able to book Members' tickets. Now I have a season ticket in the West Stand, best part, which means Upper Tier. It's in Block 4, row 17, seat 99, right above the halfway line, where the players come out. I can't see them emerge, except on the big screen, being too high up, but I can see into the directors' boxes and I always look out for Sven Goran Eriksson, manager of England, at least he was this afternoon. He usually leaves early.

The cost of my ticket for the 2002–3 season was £950, plus £4.50 admin charges. I consider it a ridiculous price, far too expensive, as the seats are cramped, you have to pay extra after the first two home cup matches, if any, which comes to a maximum of 21 games. If of course Spurs had been doing brilliantly these last few years, winning the league, playing in Europe, I would probably consider £950 a bargain price.

I went, as I always do these days, with my neighbours, Derek and Sue. Derek, who is an architect, and I used to play in the same football team, but it is Sue who is the fanatical Spurs fan, a born-again fan, who woke up one day about five years ago and bought, with her own money, two season tickets for Spurs, one for herself and one for another person – her husband, if he is lucky. It is said to be a sign of our times that more and more women are coming into football.

We take turns driving there, as public transport in that part of north London is hopeless. Today it was my turn. Back in the 1960s, I could park about a few hundred yards away from the ground, always in the same street, and I used to play a game with myself, estimating how big the crowd would be from the number of cars already there. Today, I park at least a mile away, with difficulty, which means we have to go earlier and earlier. The only good thing about a Sunday game is that you can park on a single yellow line.

We got there a good 40 minutes early, parked and walked through Bruce Castle Park towards the High Road, looking for that first wonderful sight of the stadium, the floodlights towering above, the crowds streaming down the High Road. Oh the excitement and anticipation, being part of the massed ranks, moving towards the match. Going to Wembley, that was a bigger thrill, seeing those towers, walking up Olympic Way. Will the new stadium, if it ever gets finished, ever evoke such emotions?

We parted on the corner of Park Lane, as Sue and Derek sit in the East Stand. They always go straight in and Sue puts a £1 bet on who will score the first goal. The most she has won this season has been £32. I don't like going in when the stadium is still half empty. I like to savour the atmosphere outside for as long as possible, so I stopped in the High Road to look at a stall which sells old programmes. Over the years, I have bought many pre-war Spurs programmes from the same stall-holder, when the prices were around £8. Now he has very few, and they are at least £30 each.

I then went into the Spurs megastore, the big one on the corner. There are two others, a smaller one further along the High Road, and one inside the West Stand. I like to look in the big one, just to look, not buy anything, see what Spurs tat, sorry, what souvenirs are currently on sale. A replica home shirt, long sleeved, was £35 for an adult. For a baby, the Infant Home Kit, including socks, was £30. Other attractions included woolly hats £10, baseball caps £10, towel £18, rain jacket £50, fleece lined jacket £65, ladies knickers £8 for two, ladies thong £8 for two, wall clock £18, drop earrings £16, half a bottle of champagne £25, car air freshener £2. All of course with a Spurs crest on. The current merchandising catalogue now comes to 72 glossy pages and I estimate there must be up to a thousand different items.

I then walked round the whole stadium, working my way through the crowds. There are more street stalls then ever before, a lot of them selling unofficial stuff, complete with rude anti-Arsenal slogans. I wrote down some of the words, purely as a matter of record. 'You can stick your Double up your Arse' and 'Support the Scum? I'd rather rod my dog.'

The smell of hot dogs, burgers and onions can be quite pleasant at first, when you pick up a waft from afar, but close up the stench becomes overpowering, and the sight of so many overweight, pale-faced, unhealthy people stuffing their fat faces becomes increasingly unappetising.

Once round the ground, then into the main entrance for the West Stand, down what is now called Bill Nicholson Way, after our double-winning manager of 1961, still with us. I said hello to him just a few weeks earlier. In the car park, used by players and VIP guests, was the usual assortment of Ferraris, Mercedes, BMWs and Bentleys, all top of the range.

I got my season ticket ready, looked through it for the right number, and tore it out. They announce a different number for each game, which you don't know beforehand, to deter ticket touts. They have all but disappeared anyway. You can't buy tickets on the day, and hardly any in advance. The vast majority, even those in what were once the cheaper, poorer seats, bought their season tickets back in June, as I did.

I climbed up four flights of concrete stairs to the upper tier, feeling knackered. When my knees finally go, how will I cope? There doesn't appear to be a lift. I went first to the gents, looking at some stupid posters for some sports radio station on the wall. Then I bought a programme. I don't usually, as they now cost £3 each – 50p dearer than the present Arsenal programme. They are well produced enough, 60 pages long, full colour, glossy, good photos, with pull-outs, but there's not a lot of reading and I object to all the adverts for Thomson, currently sponsors of Spurs, and Barclaycard, sponsors of the Premier League. Most of all I object to two pages being devoted to a list of firms which have bought executive boxes.

I then bought a cup of coffee in a plastic cup for £1.20, another rip off price – why do I keep buying it? The food stalls are cleaner than they were, with a bigger range, and I could have bought a smoked salmon bagel for £2.50, but it mostly still looks nasty and cheap, nowhere near as tempting as the food on sale when I went to a Real Mallorca match in Spain last year.

I had some idle chat with one or two friends, people I know only through going to the game, such as a lawyer who was active in a supporters group during the last boardroom upheaval, then five minutes before kick-off I made my way up to my seat. On the big screen, a compilation of great goals from the past was coming to an end while music blared through the PA system. I do love that first glimpse of the impossibly green, virgin, manicured grass, after all the grey and dullness of the High Road and the concrete wasteland of the bowels of the stand. It takes a moment for the eye to adjust to the greenery and to the scale of things.

Architecturally, the stadium is now properly symmetrical, all the bits new and filled in. I have often heard visiting supporters admiring our stadium. Okay, mostly from the lower divisions, playing cup-ties. The pitch looked perfect, but then Premier League pitches do these days, no bare patches, no mud baths in the goal, the way it used to be this time of the year. The crowd that day was 35,718, a full house these days, but there are plans for further extensions. It was 55,000 in the 1970s – 75,000 in the 1930s.

I shook hands with the man on my left, sitting with his grandson. He is a retired accountant, that's about all I know about him. We stood up at the sound of 'Glory, Glory Tottenham Hotspur', which always heralds the players onto the pitch, and an over excited voice welcoming everyone to White Hart Lane, 'World-Famous Home of the Spurs!' We sat down, then had to get up again for latecomers, mostly from the hospitality suites, not regular supporters. They wear smart suits, that's one clue, with big badges and flushed faces, having eaten and drunk too much.

I did have a seat in another row for a few years, but behind me was a family I grew to hate. The boys were at fee-paying schools judging by their accents, while their father sounded more norf London trader. The boys talked all the way through and shouted 'The referee's a virgin', which they thought was hilarious. So I got a move.

In the Spurs starting line-up today there were only five English players: Sheringham, Richards, King, Perry and Anderton. The others came from Germany, Yugoslavia, Ireland, Uruguay and the USA. A typical spread these days of nationalities. Three of the players were black.

Not much happened in the first ten minutes, so the crowd on the opposite stand started singing, 'Stand up if you hate Arsenal'. I turned to my friend and said, 'I'm too old to stand up.' And he replied, 'I'm too old to hate.' In the West Stand, we are the poshos, the quality, so we don't do abusive, or sing or chant songs. We clap politely at a good move, but will jump up for a goal, a Spurs goal of course.

At half-time, I watched the highlights again on the giant TV screen, one at either end, and got my little Thermos out of my little rucksack, the one I use only for football, which also contains two tangerines, a packet of throat tablets and a little fold-up umbrella. I might be superior about the burgers, but at matches I eat all the way through. I discussed the match with my accountant friend, predicted the final score, then just before the re-start I went to the lavatory again, having waited as long as possible, to avoid the crowds. But it was still packed down below, and full of smoke. Smoking is not allowed in the stadium itself, supposedly, so they smoke in the corridors.

Ten minutes before the end, people around me started to leave, which always seems mad, when the seats cost so much and anything can happen in the last ten minutes, or fifteen, as there can be up to five minutes extra added on. I've asked people why and they all say the same – to miss the traffic jams.

I got up 30 seconds before the end, but paused to watch the final whistle blow on one of the TV screens in the corridor, so missed nothing. I bought chips on the way home, cost 90p for a small portion (yes, just as bad as burgers), then sat in the car eating them while listening to BBC Radio Five Live for any match reports.

On Saturdays, I love listening to *Sports Report*, if I can race back to the car in time, which is rare, in order to hear that familiar signature tune and the first reading of the results by James Alexander Gordon. It takes me back to my childhood, waiting for the results with my father when he was an invalid in bed, writing them down, then checking his pools for him.

I had to wait for Sue and Derek as it takes them longer from their seats and Sue insists on watching the players troop off the pitch. She won £10 today, betting that Robbie Keane would get the first goal. Spurs won 2–0. My wife can always tell if Spurs have won, before I've said a word. It's the way I open the door, walk down the hall, enter the kitchen.

I like to think, when I come home, that I have been part of a greater community of football. That weekend in England, 1,334,000 people watched league games, a figure which is now some 300,000 greater than those who went to a Church of England service, thus giving football the country's biggest weekly congregation. I also like to imagine I am communing in spirit with all those who have gone before, who have watched English league games over the last 115 years. And I like to feel I have been part of the wider family of football, the millions out there across the globe who this weekend will have been watching their local team playing exactly the same game, with the same rules, using many of the same English words, going through much the same sorts of emotion.

This book is a labour of love aimed at them all, young and old, male and female, here and abroad, to tell them something about the story of football not about individual games, but the game itself. The facts and figures, goals scored, leagues won, season by season, they are all in the record books, as are the details of today's game. I'm interested here in the social and the cultural, the fashions and financial aspects of football, its development and changes. Mostly I'm trying to chart and explain how we all got from there, in the very beginning of football, to here, watching the match that I've just seen today.

BELOW Spurs programme, for the game after the Leeds match: in the 2002–3 season, it cost £3 for 60 pages.

FROM THE BEGINNINGS TO 1939

PART ONE

Taking in the history of the origins of football; the making of the rules; the coming of professionals; football equipment; players and spectators in the early decades; the arrival of football writing and football merchandise; some famous pre-war players and the rise of the football pools.

Hurrah for the
Public Schools

1

FOOTBALL, as we now know it, began in Britain, so loud hurrahs all round. It was in England in the middle of the nineteenth century, along with a little help from our Scottish friends, that the rules and tactics, language and organisations, were created. The rest of the world agrees on this. No argument there. England and particularly Scotland might not be all that brilliant at football today, no longer capable of beating everyone else as they once did, but the world acknowledges that football is a British game. We gave birth, then very kindly allowed other countries to have a go at playing it. Why?

I mean why, in England, on these shores, did it happen? Kicking a football around, in its various forms, must have been with us for, well, for ever. That seems obvious. Even just an hour or two's research will throw up examples of games of football being played in many other parts of the world, long before the nineteenth century. So what was peculiar about the conditions and forces which created it here, at that precise time? Or was it all just luck and happenstance?

The ball came first, and everyone agrees on its importance. 'In human activity,' so the American historian Barbara Tuchman has written, 'the invention of the ball may be said to rank alongside that of the wheel.' But no one has agreed on when it was invented – or discovered, for we must presume that round objects, whether of stone or natural fibre, vegetable or animal matter, were always there, just waiting to be played with, tossed or kicked about. Hard to believe that human beings, once they stood up, walked out of the cave and went hunting, did not pick up some handy sized lump and use it to throw at animals or their enemies. And when there were no enemies or animals within easy range, they would practise, to see who could hurl things furthest. Thus sport, as we now call it, was born.

Homer, the Greek poet describes in the *Odyssey* how Odysseus gets shipwrecked. After ten years of wandering, he is washed up on a beach where a 'Princess and her retinues threw their veils to the wind, struck up a game of ball.' Odysseus wakes up and sees these half-naked maidens playing with a ball, which must have been a pleasant surprise, but their shouting alarms him. 'Whose land have I list upon, what are they here – violent, savage, lawless or friendly to strangers?' In this, the first known mention of ball playing in literature, it is interesting that noise and the suggestion of violence went hand in hand with the game itself.

Homer cannot quite be trusted, as we don't exactly know when and where he lived, or even if he personally wrote the *Odyssey*, but ball playing as a womanly or courtly activity is evident in many ancient civilisations, notably in China and Japan, from wall decorations and illustrations. It's not clear what part the foot played in these early games. A Chinese writer, Li Yu (AD 50–130), mentions the use of a round ball 'like a full moon' and a goal and captains, but doesn't give us any rules.

BELOW In ancient Japan, ball playing was a courtly activity, commemorated in wall decorations, illustrations and in this case a woodcut entitled *Life at the Chiyoda Palace,* which shows Samurai warriors watching a game. The result is not known, nor even the precise rules.

There are clear records of 'foot ball' being played all over Europe in medieval times. In Italy in 1555 a form of street football was being played in Venice. It was found in Florence, too, from 1595 where it was known as calcio – and is still played there to this day. In France, Germany, Holland and Russia there are references to football from around the same time.

ENGLISH FOLK FOOTBALL

In England, the oldest references to football date back to the twelfth century when it was being played in London by school boys and young tradesmen, in each case being watched by older men, all of them getting rather excited and agitated. Again, the rules, such as they were, are not described. It was also being played in villages and rural communities all over Britain, often tied to feast days and religious ceremonies, when everyone would turn out to watch young men of one village, or one locality, compete with a rival group to force a ball through an agreed goal.

In this form of folk football, the pitch could be several miles long, stretching from one end of a village to the other, and the number of participants was unlimited, as were the rules. Kicking or holding the ball was permitted, fighting and even stabbing the opposition was common. Mostly, it was a rabble, an excuse to let off steam, settle scores, inflict damage on rivals, which was why football was regularly banned. Various monarchs over the centuries passed laws to prohibit football, amongst the earliest being in 1314 when Edward II, setting out to fight the Scots, wanted young men to concentrate on archery practice not football. James II of Scotland in 1457 banned both golf and football. Elizabeth I proclaimed that 'no foteballe play to be used or suffered within the City of London'.

Football also got itself banned by the authorities in France at various times, for the same sorts of reasons. But behind the worry about street violence was a fear of the masses getting out of hand, becoming generally rebellious, attacking property belonging to the nobs or, even worse, attacking the status quo.

A few isolated examples of early folk football continue to this day, but more often as a tourist attraction than a deadly game. It is still played annually in Ashbourne in Derbyshire where, so it is said, their game dates back to AD 217. In Kirkwall in the Orkneys, they have been playing a ball game known as 'uppies and downies' at Christmas time for centuries. In Workington in West Cumbria their ancient game, originally played between local sailors and local colliery workers, is also known as uppies and downies and is still played every Easter. There are written accounts of it in local Cumbrian papers from 1775 onwards. In the 1870s, special trains were laid on to bring in up to ten thousand spectators who watched contestants fighting for the ball through the streets, as well as in fields, rivers and the harbour. Four deaths from drowning during the game have been recorded since 1775. These days it is more peaceful, but still attracts big crowds. The traditional ball is still used, made of leather, hand-stitched by local craftsmen, but filled with flock.

Different forms of folk football were at one time common not just throughout Britain but also all over Europe, if not the world. Recent discoveries by archaeologists in Mexico have revealed a ball court in which a ball game was played in 1400 BC, with people watching and even laying bets, three of the ingredients which we like to think are dead modern.

TOFFS TAKE CHARGE

Football historians, a new academic breed that has appeared in the last ten years and is spreading fast, are competing to turn up early examples and references to football. They have already found thousands, so there is now not the slightest doubt, if ever there was, that football is very ancient. But the main questions remain – why didn't folks in all those foreign places, who had been playing football for centuries, knock it into shape, name the parts, give it a structure?

When the nineteenth century began it looked, if anything, as if football was dying out in England. Joseph Strutt in his 1801 book *Sports and Pastimes of the People of England* gives very little space to football, though he does roughly describe how it was played, with a ball being kicked between two posts. 'When the exercise becomes exceedingly violent, the players kick each other without the least ceremony.' He finishes his short description rather dismissively. 'The game was formerly much in vogue among the common people, though of late years it seems to have fallen into disrepute and is but little practised.'

This seems to have been the situation for around the next fifty years, with very few published mentions of football, until a revival slowly began. There were several elements at work in England – not directly connected with each other – in fact at first sight they could hardly be more different, which were instrumental in creating modern football, then passing it on.

FOOT BALL

Firstly, we have to hand it to those peculiar English institutions, the public schools, the great ones, the famous ones we have all heard about, such as Eton, Harrow, Charterhouse, Rugby, Marlborough, Winchester, Westminster. Most of them had been going for some time, but at the beginning of the nineteenth century they were at a low ebb: conditions were poor, education primitive, brutality rife, rebellions among the pupils common. Charterhouse in 1835 was down to 99 pupils while Harrow in 1844 had only 69.

But by the middle of the century, several forward-looking headmasters, such as Dr Arnold at Rugby and the Rev Edward Thring at Uppingham, had come along to revolutionise their schools, in both their scholarly and sporting activities. Games of football had been played in these schools, mostly fairly violent versions, and, as with folk football, they had often been banned. The new thrusting, energetic headmasters encouraged sport in all its forms, seeing it as a way of installing order and discipline and also

ABOVE Football was played in the streets of London from as early as the twelfth century, by schoolboys and young tradesmen. This is an etching of such a scene by H. Heath in 1820, several decades before the public schools took hold and stopped some of the violence and nonsense.

PREVIOUS PAGES *Football* by Thomas Webster, painted in 1839 and exhibited at the Royal Academy, perhaps the best-known football painting of the nineteenth century, yet done long before football got itself organised. The ball can be clearly seen, and appears to be of leather, with panels.

BELOW Oxford University Association football team, 1894–5. When public-school boys moved on to Oxford and Cambridge, they took their old school caps, blazers, scarves and superior poses.

providing a healthy activity for adolescent boys, distracting them from possibly more antisocial or even disgusting personal activities. Many of these reforming headmasters were clerics, muscular Christians who believed sport was good for the soul, not just the body. The rules of their traditional school games were formalised, inter-house competitions encouraged, with victors and champions recognised and rewarded.

When these public-school chaps moved on to Oxford and Cambridge, they naturally wanted to continue their school games. Some sort of football had been played by Cambridge students for many centuries. Oliver Cromwell, while a student at Sidney Sussex College from 1616–17, was a noted player, a contemporary account describing him as 'more famous for his exercise in the Fields than in the Schools, being one of the chief match-makers and players at football, cudgels or any other boystrong sport or game.'

By the mid-nineteenth century, players were arriving at Cambridge from their public schools with a definite set of rules. When they played among their fellow old boys, there were no problems. But there were endless arguments with old boys from other schools. A school situated in an urban area, such as Westminster, had a restricted playing area, football having developed in its cloisters, the ball being bounced off buttresses. They had also played in cloisters at Charterhouse. At Harrow, they kicked a ball over a building. Schools with massive playing fields would allow massive numbers on either side.

Handling, in some form, was present in most variations of old boys football. Tradition says that rugby, in which players ran while holding the ball, emerged in 1823 at Rugby when William Webb Ellis first ran with the ball, but this is partly myth, created by some Old Rugbians looking back many years later.

In football, the ball was mainly kicked, though when a ball came to you, you could catch it or knock it down by hand, but then you had to play it by foot, attempting to score a goal. The goals varied in width and had no crossbar. At Eton they referred to 'goal sticks' – not goal posts. At Harrow the goal was known as 'base'.

PLAYING BY THE RULES

At Cambridge in 1848 a group of ex-public-school boys from five different schools met to agree on a set of rules so that they could play football together. Such meetings must have happened in the past, but this was subsequently recorded by a second-year student at Trinity College, Henry Malden, who described how 'the Eton men howled at the Rugby men for handling the ball'. The meeting lasted from four in the afternoon till midnight, with other students wandering in, thinking there must be an exam on, with all the bits of paper flying around, before they agreed what the rules should be.

Alas, no copy of these rules has survived, but the two basic matters of contention at that meeting, and other similar meetings, were about handling and hacking. Handling was generally agreed to be okay, as long as you didn't then run while holding the ball. Hacking appeared to cover everything from tackling another player to physical assault, bringing him down violently, whether he had the ball or not. Some preferred this no-holds-barred approach, saying it was a man's game. Some contemporary accounts of playing football at this time cite arguments on school fields about the ball which would end with someone saying, 'oh, damn the ball, let's get on with the game.' But younger, more modern players, wanted hacking so defined that it allowed tackling but banned assault.

Present at that Cambridge meeting was an Old Etonian, Charles Thring, brother of the Rev Edward Thring, headmaster of Uppingham. Charles Thring went on to be a house master at the same school and in 1862 he published the first known set of rules of football, which he wanted his school footballers to follow. He called it *The Simplest Game* and managed to get it all down to 250 words and just ten rules.

Rule One was about scoring. 'A goal is scored whenever the ball is forced through the goal and under the bar, except [if] it be thrown by hand.' So, right from the beginning, Diego Maradona would have been penalised.

Rule Two said that 'Hands may be used only to stop a ball and place it on the ground before the feet.' In other words, you couldn't run with it, but anyone could handle it. Rule Three finally outlawed hacking. 'Kicks must be aimed only at the ball.'

Rule Four is a bit of a mystery and it's hard at this distance of time to be sure what it was they were outlawing. 'A Player may not kick the ball whilst in the air.' Did this refer to the player or the ball being in the air? If the latter, it might have had something to do with the need to bring the ball down by hand, then play it with the feet. If it referred to a player, then this could have been an early hint of the present-day law which penalises feet lifted dangerously high.

Rule Five was also about violence. 'No tripping or heel kicking allowed.' As we all know, there is fat chance of this ever being eliminated from the game, whatever the rules.

Rule Six was about a ball going out of play – which had to be kicked back in, not thrown in. Rule Seven was about goal kicks, Rule Eight about players having to stand six paces away at kick-off and Rule Nine concerned offside. The offside rule was very similar to rugby's, making any forward pass illegal.

Rule Ten, the last on Thring's list, was again about violence, 'No charging is allowed when player is out of play.'

In these ten simple rules, there was no mention of the ball, size of goals, area of pitch, boots, referee, number of players on each side or how long a match would last. Either the players for whom Thring was writing out his rules had already accepted them, or more likely they agreed certain things each time, according to who and what turned up.

There was also no reference to any penalties for infringements of these rules, but then perhaps they were not thought necessary. N. L. Jackson in his book *Association Football*, published in 1899, looks back to this golden age. 'In the very early days of the game, when it was chiefly confined to old public-school boys, the laws were strictly observed, any infringement being purely accidental. This was doubtless due to that honourable understanding which is cultivated among boys at the better-class schools and which prevents them taking unfair advantage of an opponent.' So that was all right then.

The absence of a stated number of players on each side is more surprising. During these early years, and early versions of the laws, when arguments were still raging about hacking and handling, there does not seem to have been much discussion about the number of players on each side. In folk football, there were no limits. It all depended on how many turned up. When the public schools and Oxbridge players began to organise themselves, they didn't worry much either. In the 1850s, teams often had 12, 15 and even 20 players a side, though it was still left to the captains of either side to decide on exact numbers.

By the 1860s, the number had settled down to 11-a-side and this became, from then on, normal practice. But why 11? Such an odd number. Ten would have been neater, the fingers of two hands. You can't say they were thinking of ten, plus a goalkeeper making 11, as the goalkeeper was not then the separate player he is today. Perhaps they just pinched it from cricket. Yet rugby, when it finally decided on its rules, chose 15.

THE FA IS BORN

The vital meeting, which we now consider the beginning of modern football, took place in London on October 26, 1863, at the Freemason's Tavern in Great Queen Street, Lincoln's Inn Fields. Twelve different football clubs came together to form an association 'with the object of establishing a definite set of rules for the regulation of the game', calling themselves the Football Association.

All of the 12 clubs were based in the London area, mostly consisting of old public-school boys and Oxbridge graduates, many of them clerics. They were not attempting to control the game, but to agree on the same set of rules when playing each other. The announcement of the Association's formation merited only a short news item in *The Times*.

Their original discussions were based on Thring's simple rules and those which had been created earlier in Cambridge, but it took them several heated meetings before they could agree on their own rules – and the main bones of contention were once again handling and hacking. Mr Campbell of the Blackheath Football Club was strongly in favour of each, especially hacking.

'Hacking is the true football game and if you look into the Winchester records you will find that in former years men were so wounded that they were actually carried off the field. I think if you do away with it you will do away with all the courage and pluck of the game, and I will be bound to bring over a lot of Frenchmen who would beat you with a week's practice ...'

His last remark was greeted with some laughter, as remarks about effeminate Frenchmen often still are, but he was serious in his attempts to retain hacking in its more physical forms. But when it came to a vote, Mr Campbell was defeated by thirteen votes to four.

The FA's first set of rules, published in December 1863, banned tripping, hacking, holding and pushing an adversary, and also running while holding the ball, but there still existed a 'fair catch', similar to a mark in rugby, whereby if you made a clean catch, you earned your team a free-kick.

Mr Campbell was not at all pleased at the disappearance of bodily tackling, and at the next meeting he declared that his club, Blackheath, had withdrawn from the FA. This was an important withdrawal as it signalled a significant split between the two embryo football codes. The Rugby Football Union was not officially formed till 1871, but this was the point at which they went their separate ways.

At first, the FA's version of football's rules was not accepted by all clubs. In Sheffield, where a football club had been founded in 1857 by some old Etonians, they continued to play according to their own rules. They were in fact much the same, except for some details of the offside rule, and in 1866 the London association managed quite amicably to play a game against the Sheffield association.

The game in the mid-1860s would still have struck us as fairly strange, not to say comical. Nine out of the eleven would have been chasing after the ball, leaving only two defenders. At the head of the charge was the best dribbler, followed by the 'backers up', who would dribble till knocked off the ball, sometimes quite violently. Dribbling was often highly skilled and greatly admired. The other team would then charge the other way down the field. A bit like playground football. Any sort of pass to someone ahead of you on your own side resulted in offside, so passing was virtually non-existent. A ball could be caught by hand, but then had to be played by foot. A ball out of play, or over the goal-line, resulted in a mad dash, because the first side to get to it and touch it down got possession. Throw-ins were one handed, in a straight line, as in rugby. Whoever was acting as goalkeeper could be charged and bundled into the net – except there wasn't a net or even a crossbar at first, just a tape.

Catching the ball disappeared in 1866, and that same year the offside rules were changed. You were onside if three of the opposition, including the goalie, were nearer their goal-line than any in your team. This led to more people defending, the normal formation turning into just five forwards, with three in the middle, two at the back.

In 1870, Sheffield agreed to abide by the FA, so the FA's rules became uniform throughout England. Queen's Park in Glasgow, Scotland's first club, founded in 1867, had their own version of the rules for a while, but Scottish players based in London happily played against an English team in 1870. The Scottish FA was formed in 1873, and within ten years all four of the home countries had agreed on the same code.

So the English public school boys and Oxbridge graduates had done all football lovers a jolly good turn, knocking a rough, folksy, violent, disorganised, amorphous ball game into shape, creating uniform rules which everyone accepted. The result was quite an exciting, enjoyable spectacle to watch, and, best of all, provided excellent manly fun for healthy young gentlemen to take part in.

ABOVE Mark Witham, one of the earliest Sheffield players, represented Sheffield against London and Glasgow. He later became a professional with Sheffield United.

Enter the
Working Classes

2

NOTICE SOMETHING MISSING in 1870 from football, as we know it and love it today? Lots of things still to come of course, in the way of rules, tactics and equipment, but it's hard to believe now that for the first decade or so of organised football there were no competitions. No pots or prizes were awarded, no points were played for, except the honour of the club or school. It was taking part that mattered most.

Yet it seems such a natural human urge to say, 'I am the best, I am the champion, I thumped everyone else and got pots to prove it.' In folk football, the same game was played at the same time every year against the same people. It was remembered who won last year, but it was what happened rather than the exact score that got recorded. At the big public schools, their games were mainly internal, among themselves. Travelling, for groups or individuals, was of course pretty difficult, until the middle of the nineteenth century and the arrival of the railways.

FA SET CUP CHALLENGE

It was the secretary of the FA, Charles Alcock, who came up with the idea of the Challenge Cup in 1871. He suggested that all the clubs who were members of the FA, and had been playing endless friendlies against each other, should be invited to compete for a trophy on a knock-out basis. He borrowed the idea from his old school, remembering how the houses at Harrow competed with each other to be Cock House.

Fifty clubs were eligible, but only 15 entered in the first year, 1872. The final was held at the Oval cricket ground in London between the Royal Engineers and the Wanderers, a side containing some of the best players from the public schools and Oxbridge, their star player being the

OPPOSITE Folk football was for the working classes, a chance for them to let off steam, kick a few enemies, run riot in the streets or the village. In Workington, West Cumbria, a form of folk football called uppies and downies dates back to at least the eighteenth century and is still played today, every Easter. In the early decades, four deaths from drowning were recorded during the game. Curley Hill, holding the ball, a well-known Workington player in 1908, managed to stay alive and on the winning side and is pictured here holding the ball.

ABOVE The Hon. F. A. Kinnaird, later president of the FA, played in nine FA finals, firstly for the Wanderers, then Old Etonians.

BELOW Charles Alcock – the most important innovator in the early history of football. He created the FA Cup, remembering how at his old school, Harrow, the houses had competed to be Cock House. He thought up the first international, between England and Scotland, and did some of the earliest football writing.

Revd R. W. S. Vidal, known as 'The Prince of Dribblers'. One of the Royal Engineers, Lt Cresswell, broke his collar bone after ten minutes, but gallantly played on to the end. The Wanderers won 1–0 before a crowd of 3,000, and the FA Challenge Cup, made at a cost of £20, was presented to their captain C. W. Alcock. Yes, the same, the FA's secretary who had thought up the competition. Football, in those early days, was organised by chums for chums.

In 1873, the Cup Final was between Oxford University and the Wanderers. Kick-off was deliberately arranged for mid-morning so that all the players and spectators could rush off afterwards and watch the Oxford–Cambridge Boat Race, which gives a clue to the background of the sort of people who were playing and watching football in the 1870s. For the first 11 years, from 1872 to 1883, all the winners were old boys' teams from London and the South, such as Old Etonians, Oxford University and Old Carthusians.

The Hon. Arthur Kinnaird played in nine finals, five of them on the winning side, firstly for the Wanderers and then for Old Etonians. He was a huge, red-bearded giant of a man, with a personality to match, a member of an aristocratic family with a large estate in Perthshire. After the 1882 victory, as part of his celebrations, he stood on his head in front of the stands. On the pitch, he was known for his fierce tackling and violent charging. The supporters loved him, as they usually do, when committed players get stuck in. On arriving for one game in his own carriage, his fans took the horses away and pulled his coach by hand to the players' entrance.

Sir Francis Marindin, the President of the FA, visited Kinnaird's mother one day and found her very worried about her son. 'I'm afraid that one of these days Arthur will come home with a broken leg,' said Lady Kinnaird.

'Never fear, madam,' reassured Marindin. 'It will not be his own.'

This story appeared in several publications around the turn of the century, though in some versions Marindin was visiting Kinnaird's wife, not his mother, but the exchange is the same. Kinnaird himself went on to become President of the FA for many years, an earl and also High Commissioner of the Church of Scotland.

THE RISE OF THE NORTH

In that 1882 Cup Final, Kinnaird and Old Etonians, beat Blackburn Rovers – the first team from outside the South who had made it to the Cup Final. The next year, 1883, Old Etonians were in the final again, but this time they got beaten by Blackburn Olympic. Never again did an amateur team, or a team of southern ex-public-school boys, the people who had created football, win the FA Cup. The North had arrived.

Several of these new northern clubs had been formed by ex-public-school boys, going out into the world, or clerics, taking their mission to industrial towns. Bolton Wanderers, Blackpool, Everton, Birmingham City and Wolves all had their origins in church teams. Some were factory owners, encouraging their workers to play healthy games, imposing the rules of football, as laid down by the FA, the old forms of folk or village football having long died out in most places. With the Industrial Revolution, people had moved to towns and forgotten their traditional pastimes. But once the Industrial Revolution had settled down, new forms of urban life and work and then leisure appeared, enabling the working classes to pick up the baton of football once again, taking it over from the more leisured, flannelled, amateur, southern classes.

It was the excitement of the FA Cup – and other local, regional and county cup competitions that followed – which created the crowds, with more people wanting to watch than take part. The idea of a mass audience had not existed until the northern and Midland urban clubs arrived on the scene. Mass audiences came from massive factories, massed industrial

LEFT Blackburn Rovers got to the FA Cup Final in 1882, the first northern club to do so, but were beaten by Kinnaird's Old Etonians. However, they made it onto a commemorative tin lid, along with other late-nineteenth century super star sportsmen.

towns and back-to-back mass housing. The crowd for that first Cup Final, held in 1872, had been only three thousand, but by the time Blackburn Rovers won the Cup for the third year running in 1886, the crowd had risen to fifteen thousand.

A vital element in big crowds coming out in the North to watch big football games was the introduction of Saturday afternoons as a half-day off from work. Various Factory Acts from the 1840s onwards, spurred on by union agitation, had begun to create shorter working hours, especially in the textile industry. Other industries slowly followed. By the 1860s and 1870s, most factories let their workers – though not their clerical staff – off at one o'clock on Saturdays. Many went straight to the pub, to get refreshed, then to the match, to be entertained and forget their work.

The other factor that helped create mass crowds was improvement in transport. Regular, cheap trains into Manchester, Birmingham, Newcastle,

Sheffield and other urban centres brought supporters from up to 20 miles away who would never otherwise have thought of going to watch a city-centre-based football club. For big games, against clubs from rival cities, they were prepared to travel much greater distances. Inside these cities, there was an excellent system of trams, taking fans right to the entrance of the football ground. Players themselves would not have been able to play in faraway towns for cup ties without the improvements in transport. The invention of the telegraph and the introduction of a cheap penny post also helped football to expand, making communications and arrangements much easier.

No gate money was taken from any watching supporters when the public schools first played. Why should it? They could easily afford their own sports fields and their own equipment. The players and the spectators were equally well off. But when football clubs sprang up in the North, they had to hire a ground or a playing field. It's true that one of the joys of football, and a major reason for its worldwide popularity, is that it can be played anywhere, on almost any surface, from beaches to cobbled back streets. All you need is a ball, of sorts. Everything else can be improvised. But once you have real competitions, a slightly better surface and a proper arena are needed, which have to be paid for.

The more money clubs could take in, the easier it was to hire a better pitch, better equipment, and also allow their players some modest expenses. Just for travelling, of course, or to buy themselves a pair of boots. In these northern towns, the players were mostly factory workers, so the next stage was to reimburse them for their efforts, which seemed only fair, offering small sums in lieu of the time they had been forced to take off in order to train or travel. The FA Cup of course, if you did well, meant much more travelling than in the days of local friendlies.

THE ERA OF SHAMATEURISM

Clubs soon realised that one way of winning was to attract the best players from other clubs – and the best way to attract them was to pay better 'expenses'. Clubs also found that with success came bigger crowds, more income, therefore more money to attract even better players. All very obvious now, but the process happened gradually, stage by stage.

Professionalism started in the North of England – but the first professionals were Scottish-born players. In Scotland, as the game expanded, and workers' teams from Glasgow and elsewhere were formed, they developed a slightly different style of playing. Instead of charging forward in a gang, following whomever was the team's star dribbler, they found they could make just as much progress by passing the ball. When English clubs from Lancashire and Yorkshire went up to Scotland to play games, as they did when there were no cup games, they very often got well beaten. The first Scotland v England international was held in 1872, another of Alcock's brilliant initiatives, and was a goalless draw. But after that, Scotland usually thumped England. Of the next 12 games, between 1873 and 1884, Scotland won nine while England won only twice.

In the FA Cup of 1879, a minor sensation was caused when Darwen, a small-time cotton workers' club from industrial Lancashire, held the mighty Old Etonians to a 5–5 draw in the Fourth Round. OE's went on to win the replay 6–2, so normal, amateur, public-school values were maintained, but it came out that Darwen's two star players, Fergus Suter and James Love, were both Scottish. How come they were playing for an English club? Some mystery here.

It was revealed that while playing with their Scottish club, Partick Thistle, founded 1876, on an English tour, the two had played against Darwen – and played so well that they had been persuaded to go missing, not to return to Glasgow with the rest of the team. The persuasions were said to include the promise of well-paid but not too arduous jobs in the local cotton mill, plus money in their boots after every game.

This was the first known case of players receiving any money for playing football, but it had clearly been happening for some time, with the better-off northern clubs able to offer under-the-counter, in-your-socks, payments and inducements. All against the FA rules, of course, as association football was strictly an amateur game, which was how the FA's founders saw it and how, so they believed, God and nature had intended.

The southern, amateur, old boys' clubs were most upset, said it was the end of the game as they knew it and refused to play against any team which included professionals as it 'degraded respectable gentlemen'. It wasn't simply an anti-commercial, anti-monetary attitude based on class prejudice, but a genuine belief that the game would be tainted, played in a different spirit, in a different way, once winning at all costs became the overriding factor.

It looked as if football might well fall apart or at least split, with the northern and Midlands clubs admitting publicly they were paying players.

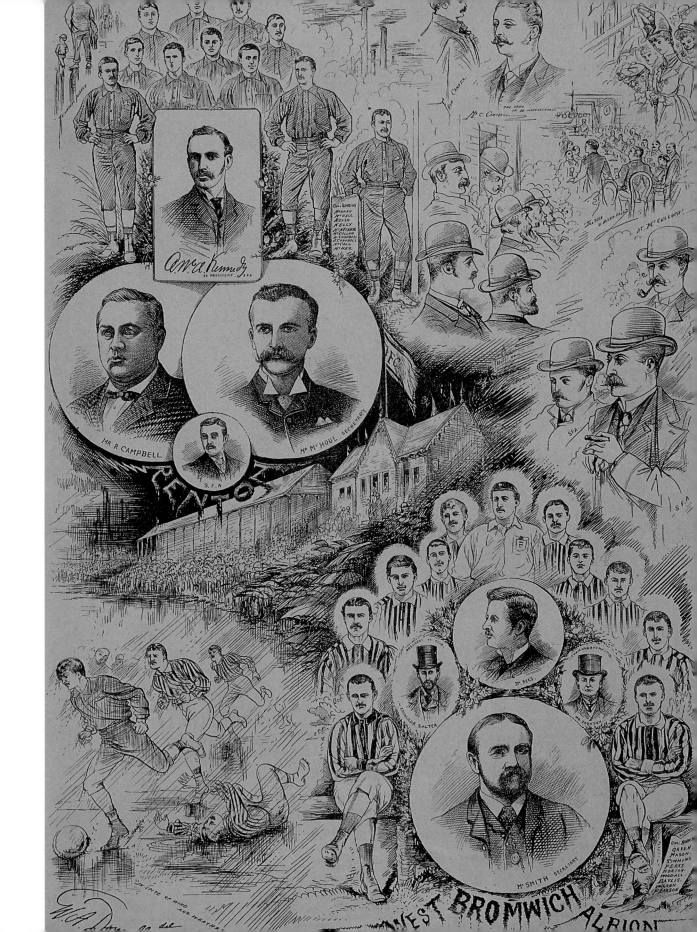

ABOVE Wolverhampton Wanderers, another founder member of the Football League and a leading professional club – yet in their 1895–6 team photograph, not all were wearing shin pads, three did not have their arms folded and one had even turned his chair back to front. Uniform photographs, with all teams lined up in much the same way, were yet to come.

All the professional clubs might well have left the FA to form their own body but for the good sense and calm approach of Charles Alcock, the FA's Secretary. Personally, he preferred the amateur game and its values, but he defended the professionals, refusing to see them as the 'utter outcasts some people represent them to be'. He realised that professionalism was inevitable for the growth of the game.

The arguments about shamateurism went on for some years, and various clubs, such as Preston North End, got chucked out of the FA Cup when it was alleged they were using professional players. Bolton Wanderers were also accused, but managed to cover their tracks – then later openly admitted it.

In 1885 the FA gave in to the inevitable, and by a two-thirds majority, professionals were declared legal. In Scotland, despite the existence of professional Scots elsewhere, professionalism was still not allowed, partly due to the influence and power of Queen's Park FC, which always remained resolutely amateur. But soon the big Scottish clubs, like Rangers, founded 1873, and then Celtic, founded 1887, were employing shamateurs. 'You might as well attempt to stop the flow of Niagara with a kitchen chair as to endeavour to stem the tide of professionalism,' said the Celtic representative at the SFA's 1893 AGM, the meeting at which Scotland followed England in finally allowing professionalism.

The FA had thus cleverly and sensibly kept control of the whole game in England, both amateur and professional, but for once they missed out on the next important development in the game. At this distance it seems so obvious a development it is hard to believe they had not introduced it back in 1863, when the FA first met, but it probably needed professionalism to come in first, before it became so glaringly obvious.

Having professional players meant regular wages had to be paid out – but how could clubs guarantee a regular income when they depended so heavily on the FA Cup? Once they were knocked out, that was it for another season. It was back to endless friendlies, some of which were arranged at the last minute against much smaller clubs and liable to be cancelled. Yet the clubs by now had grown so much, crowds for big games up to ten thousand, with a dozen or so professional players to be paid.

Many of the gents at the FA were still hankering after the innocent, amateur days of old when the game was played for fun and sport not money. They resented the rise and increasing power of the northern professional clubs and gave little thought to their problems, leaving the professional clubs to find their own solution.

LEAGUE FOOTBALL AT LAST

In March 1888, a Scotsman called William McGregor of the Aston Villa club in Birmingham sent a letter to some of the leading clubs. 'Every year it is becoming more and more difficult for football clubs of any standing to meet their friendly engagements. The consequence is that at the last moment, through cup-tie interferences, clubs are compelled to take on teams who will not attract the public. I beg to tender the following suggestion as a means of getting over the difficulty: that ten or twelve of the most prominent clubs in England combine to arrange home and away fixtures each season.'

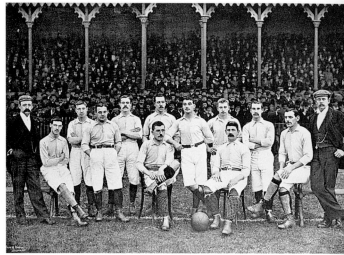

ABOVE Various forms of team line-ups were tried in the early decades, with sometimes dazzling effects. Left to right, Newcastle United in 1908 display their stripes and a surprisingly large pool of players; Blackburn Rovers, 1896, are rather languid and superior; Sunderland in 1896 had a front row bent at an angle, perhaps imagining they were public-school boys; Bradford City in 1908 had got their players into two very neat professional rows with all arms folded. Well done.

McGregor had experienced the problems at first-hand with Villa, so he recalled in a book some years later, when for five Saturdays in a row games had been called off for various reasons, thus disappointing supporters, making printed fixture cards a nonsense and threatening bankruptcy as weekly wages still had to be paid. He suggested a meeting at Anderton's Hotel in Fleet Street, London, on Friday, March 23, 1888, knowing that lots of the big clubs would be down in London for the Cup Final at the Oval, between West Bromwich Albion and Preston North End. At this first meeting, it became clear that no southern club was interested in the new idea. A few weeks later, a second meeting was held in Manchester, at the Royal Hotel, and the establishment of a league of 12 teams was approved – Aston Villa, Accrington Stanley, Blackburn Rovers, Bolton Wanderers, Burnley, Derby County, Everton, Notts County, Preston North End, Stoke City, West Bromwich Albion and Wolverhampton Wanderers. All were professional clubs. Six were from Lancashire, the rest from around the Midlands.

In his memoirs, McGregor says he was not sure what to call the new collective. 'I was personally not favourable at first to the title "League" as just at that time the word was disliked on account of the doings of the Irish Land League. I believe I suggested "The Association Football Union" but it was feared that this would not be pleasing to the Rugby Union. Despite my little antipathy, the title "The Football League" was adopted.'

All the clubs agreed to remain members of the FA, but they were now in charge of their own professional league. The FA's headquarters have always

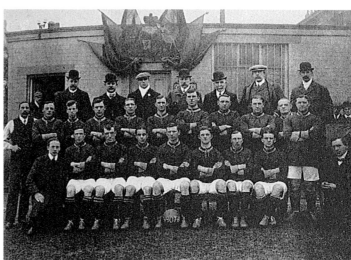

been in London, originally in Holborn, then Chancery Lane, before moving to Lancaster Gate in 1929. The Football League was always based in the North, in deepest Lancashire.

The world's first football league started off on September 8, 1888, with the 12 clubs promising to field their best available team. Two points were to be awarded for a win, but it took them a few weeks, with the season already in progress, before they decided a draw would earn one point. Preston North End won that first league, going unbeaten for a whole season.

In 1892, a second division was created, again with no Southern teams. The only teams not from the North West, North East or Midlands were Grimsby and Lincoln City.

By 1893, in just 30 years, the game of professional football was firmly established and being played very much as it is today. While a game played in 1863 would have struck us as pretty funny, with some weird rules, touch downs and handling, players charging up and down with no apparent formation, by the mid-1890s we had passing as well as dribbling, teams arranged into defenders, half-backs and forwards. Corner kicks were introduced in 1873, crossbars in 1875, two-handed throws in 1882, penalty kicks and nets in 1891.

And referees had appeared. Originally, when public schools played each other, they each brought along their own umpire who shouted or waved his handkerchief to attract attention should he spot an infringement. A referee was someone who stood on the sidelines, ready to arbitrate between them, though he was rarely needed with gentlemen players. When it got more serious and professional, the independent referee was given sole charge – and from 1878 he was armed with a whistle.

So, the reason football began here when it did was because of the great nineteenth-century public schools, peculiarly English and without counterparts abroad. The reasons why it then because so popular, with money and mass appeal, were related to the effects of the Industrial Revolution, which began here in Britain, in the North and the Midlands.

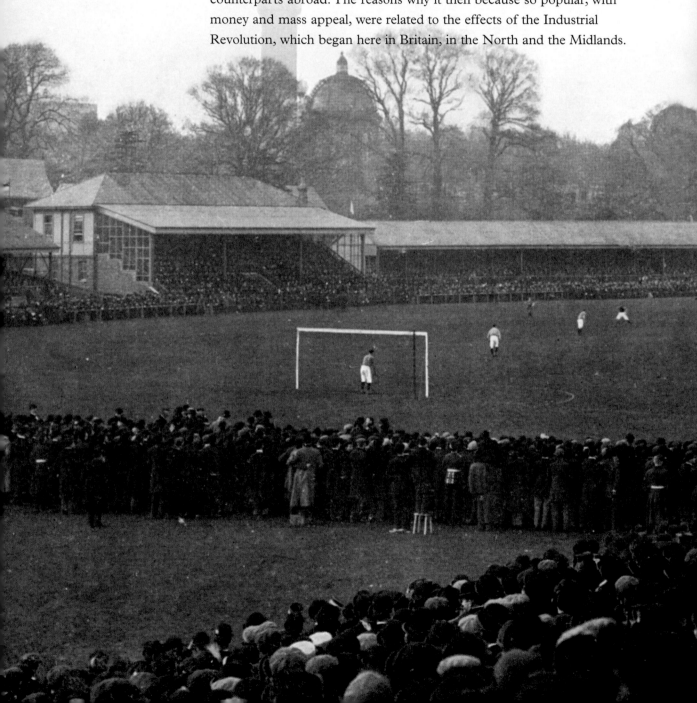

The arrival of the second element in the birth of football, the working classes, heralded the beginning of the decline of the first, the public-school, Oxbridge, amateur influence. But they left us with one other inheritance.

In the 1880s, an Oxford undergraduate called Charles Wreford-Brown, later a star player with Corinthians and an official of the Football Association, was asked by some friends one morning if he was going to play association football or rugby football in the afternoon. He said he was going to play soccer not rugger. As far as is known, he was the first to use the word 'soccer', a bit of a visual wordplay, taking it from 'association'. That's the story anyway. The public schools were not just responsible for the rules, the FA Cup and internationals, but also a word that lingers on to this day.

BELOW Aston Villa v Everton in the 1897 Cup Final at Crystal Palace which was watched by 66,000. Note the 'bra'-shaped markings of the goal area, and the penalty area which stretched the full width of the pitch. They were changed to the present day markings in the 1901–2 season. It's the one way of dating early football photos.

Equipment:
Bring on the Balls

3

HOMER DOES NOT TELL US what the princess's ball was made of. Perhaps it was some sort of fruit or nut which happened to be round. Ball shapes do occur in nature, though they are not always easy to use. Try kicking a coconut. When I was working on the biography of Dwight Yorke, then playing for Manchester United, I went to Tobago to see his mother. She told me that when Dwight was young he used to play in the backyard with a calabash. I didn't quite know what a calabash was, so one of his brothers took me out into a field to find one. It's a gourd from a calabash tree, shaped a bit like a coconut, but hollow and very light. Much easier to play with than a coconut, but it still hurts your toe when you kick it.

Or perhaps early balls were made of natural rubber. Columbus, on his second voyage to the West Indies in 1493, observed the locals in Cuba playing with something which bounced so high he thought it was alive, then later discovered it was rubber.

Or it could have been made of leather, filled with straw or flock. Leather was used by primitive man for clothing and also for carrying water. Old leather buckets do look like early footballs, the panels carefully stitched together, a bit like the balls still used in Workington for their folk football.

In medieval records, when football was being banned, the word 'leather' is often used as a synonym for the ball – a usage which continued into the early decades of real football, according to newspaper reports of late-nineteenth-century and early-twentieth-century matches. The leather ball in folk football was often stuffed, which meant it hardly bounced. That didn't matter much in such a violent game, but from very early days, leather was also used to encase a ball made from a pig's or cow's bladder. On its own, an animal's bladder would hardly have survived being kicked. We don't know when a bladder was first inflated, tied with a knot and then shoved inside a leather casing in order to protect it, but that was clearly a vital development. There is a German engraving dating from 1630 which shows a ball being blown up with what looks exactly like a modern pump.

The boys at Charterhouse, founded 1611, had a song that dates back at least to 1794 in which they celebrate the bladder. 'I challenge all the men alive / To say they e're the gladder / Than boys all striving who should kick / Most wind out of the bladder.'

In that 1801 book by Strutt on English sports, in which he dismissed football as passé, he describes the ball. 'Commonly made of a blown bladder, and cased with leather ... the object of each party is to drive it through the goal of their antagonists.'

The balls children played with, until the mid-nineteenth century, were either made of natural rubber, which bounced too high to be much good for foot games, or were leather-covered bladders, which were expensive. It was Charles Goodyear, the American inventor, who is credited with revolutionising the ball, and therefore most ball games. In 1854 his rubber-cored ball, coated with other materials, won a gold medal at the international exhibition in Paris. It was much easier to play with and helped change the nature and popularity of golf and tennis – as well as football. Boy footballers, playing in the streets and not able to afford a proper inflated football, could always use a cheap tennis ball.

The early rules of football, from the beginning of the FA in 1863, did not mention the ball, apart from stating that it must be a sphere. Footballs at the time could be as big and heavy as medicine balls, shaped like a peeled orange, with a patch at either end. In 1872, the FA laid down the dimensions, between 27 and 29 inches in circumference, and from then on they were all roughly the same size and weight and texture.

Real leather footballs, with bladders, stayed with us for the next hundred years, till it all changed. They were hellish to head, particularly if by chance you headed the lace bit, which could cut your head, and in wet weather they got heavier and heavier as the leather soaked up the rain. In 2002, a coroner said it was likely that the death of Jeff Astle at the age of 59, a well-known West Bromwich Albion centre forward of the 1960s and 1970s, was caused by 'repeated small traumas to the brain' brought about by heading leather footballs. The problem was not in fact the balls, which when dry were no heavier than modern balls, but what happened to them in bad weather.

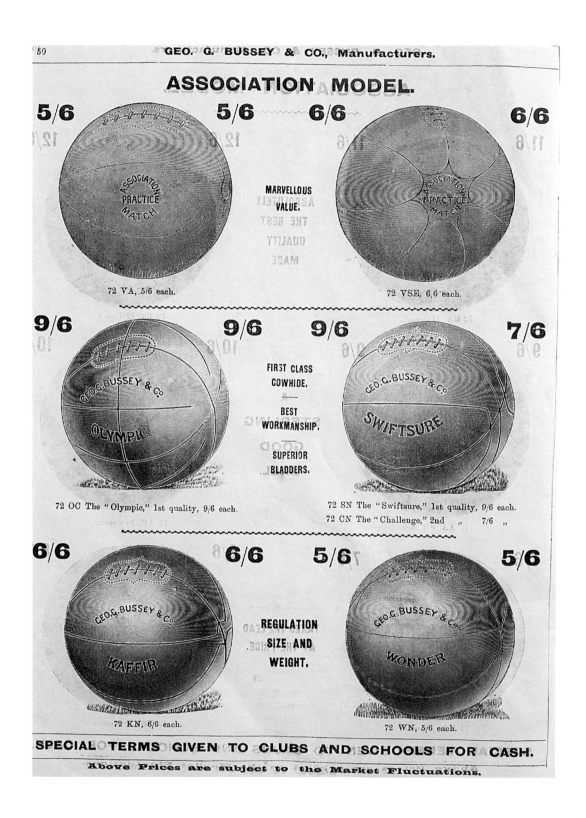

50   GEO. G. BUSSEY & CO., Manufacturers.

ASSOCIATION MODEL.

5/6   5/6   6/6   6/6

MARVELLOUS
VALUE.

72 VA, 5/6 each.   72 VSE, 6/6 each.

9/6   9/6   9/6   7/6

FIRST CLASS
COWHIDE.

BEST
WORKMANSHIP.

SUPERIOR
BLADDERS.

72 OC The "Olympic," 1st quality, 9/6 each.   72 SN The "Swiftsure," 1st quality, 9/6 each.
                                                72 CN The "Challenge," 2nd   „   7/6   „

6/6   6/6   5/6   5/6

REGULATION
SIZE AND
WEIGHT.

72 KN, 6/6 each.   72 WN, 5/6 each.

SPECIAL TERMS GIVEN TO CLUBS AND SCHOOLS FOR CASH.

Above Prices are subject to the Market Fluctuations.

FOOTBALL FASHION VICTORIAN STYLE

What did early footballers wear to play football? The original players, being public-school types, wore the gaily coloured, patterned jerseys they wore for games at school, often denoting their individual houses. Some of the designs were as dazzling as those worn by today's jockeys. Stripes were very popular, as worn by the young gents of Harrow in that marvellous 1870s photograph, head to toe, like pyjamas or as if they were high-class convicts.

In Routledge's *Handbook to Football*, published in 1867, teams were advised to play in different colours. 'If it can be previously so arranged, to have one side with striped jerseys of one colour, say red, and the other with another, say blue. This prevents confusion and wild attempts to wrest the ball from your neighbour. I have often seen this done and heard the invariable apology – "I beg your pardon, I thought you were on the opposite side ..."'

The public-school players were clearly very proud of their shirts, posing for photographs in their best and cleanest outfits. You never see photographs from the early years of any footballers looking filthy and muddy. Cameras of the time could not cope with action shots, so they trooped into studios or the photographer set up a shot in the cloisters. They all wanted to look their best and let the world see their school or club colours, proof that they were in the First XI.

Northern teams could not at first afford the proper gear and played in any old clothes, even reasonably well-known teams. An 1870s description of some players at Darwen noticed they were wearing ordinary trousers, with braces and unmatching shirts. 'Some who boasted knickerbockers had these useful garments made from old trousers cut down.' But by the 1880s, with cup successes and professionalism creeping in, the northern clubs followed the public-school fashion for strong, distinctive shirts, creating flashes of brightness in otherwise drab, urban landscapes.

We assume today that all well-known clubs have had their team colours for ever, which in a sense they have, the older clubs playing in the same colours they used 100 years ago, but in the very early years, colours and designs often changed quite frequently. Heart of Midlothian, in their team photo for 1876, look very ducky with their white shirts, a cross between matelots and oarsmen, with a red heart on their left breast. It was a couple of years later that they settled down into their now familiar maroon and white shirts. Bolton Wanderers in 1884 were wearing white shirts with red spots, which was said at the time to 'have a tendency to make the men

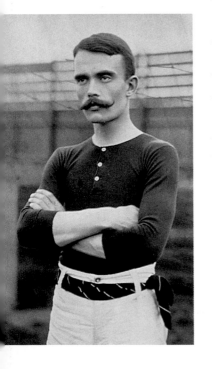

BELOW Early players often wore a belt or, failing that, a pretty sash in order to keep their trousers up and also make them look strong and dashing.

LEFT Stripes were very popular, as worn by the young gents of Harrow in the 1870s, though it was not so common to be dressed quite so stripily, tops as well as bottoms, and even hats, making them seem like high-class convicts rather than high-class public-school boys.

appear much larger'. That same year they appeared in a cup match in salmon pink while their opponents that day, Notts County, wore chocolate and blue. Yummy. Good enough to eat. Everton at one time played in black with a scarlet sash. The latest fashions in football wear were often commented upon. Blackburn Rovers, for a match against Sunderland in 1889, were reported to have 'looked in their pretty blue and white panelled jerseys a very smart lot'.

Northern professional teams, once they were successful, were just as concerned about looking good as the well-bred amateurs. Before the FA Cup Final of 1888 against West Brom, Preston North End wanted to be photographed before the kick-off with the cup, so confident were they of winning. They explained that after the game they would all be dirty, which would ruin the pic, but the referee would not allow it. 'Had not you better win first?' he said. West Brom in fact beat them, one of the earliest ever cup upsets.

The designs of the early shirts varied – some had collars, some didn't, some had buttons like old-fashioned vests, while others laced up at the neck.

ANDY WILSON

W. H. SMITH

F. MOSS

J. MARSHALL

BOB KELLY

A. GR...

ABOVE AND OPPOSITE The designs of the early shirts were varied – some had collars, some didn't, some had buttons like old-fashioned vests, while others laced up at the neck. The lace-up style was very popular right up to the 1930s.

The lace-up style was popular right up to the 1930s. In the 2002 World Cup, it was noticeable that Uruguay were the only team wearing lace-up shirts, the message being what a traditional footballing nation we are.

Shirts were baggy at first, rather heavy, more like rugby jerseys, but got lighter over the years. They also got tighter when professionals started playing. For some reason, in some clubs a tight shirt was a mark of a professional, distinguishing him from his amateur colleagues. Green never took off as a colour, except in Scotland, thanks to the Celtic and Hibernian. In England, there is no major team that plays in green – the nearest being Plymouth Argyle. In England, green was generally considered an unlucky colour.

In Cassell's *Book of Sports and Pastimes*, published in 1892, there is some help on what to wear. 'The most convenient dress for Football consists of a tight-fitting jersey and knickerbockers and stockings of the same colour as the jersey. Some of the more prominent Association clubs, however, wear a flannel shirt instead of a jersey. This costume is perhaps more picturesque.'

Football is included in a section marked 'Manly Games and Exercises', and so it should be. 'Was there ever a football player who has not gloried in the hacks and bruises which are certain to result from a well-fought game?

The statement once made that Waterloo was won on the playing fields of Eton is not absurdly exaggerated one for the grand old English games, and Football in particular, are admirably calculated to engender those sterling qualities which have won for British soldiers so many hardly contested fights.'

In the early decades, goalkeepers wore the same shirt as the rest of his team, which made things difficult when it came to a goalmouth melee. In 1909, in order to help referees, the FA decreed that goalkeepers must wear scarlet or royal-blue shirts. In 1912, royal green was added to the list, and became the most popular colour. By this time, the fashion for goalkeepers was to wear heavy polo-neck jerseys, as opposed to shirts, a style which continued until the 1950s.

SHORTS, KNICKERS AND TASSELLED CAPS

There were no shorts at first. Everyone played in long knickerbockers, made of wool or fleece, usually tied by buttons below the knee, halfway down the calf. Lord Kinnaird was always in white knickerbockers, as were most of the early players, which must have been hard to wash, but then public-school boys usually had staff to look after such things.

Knickerbockers got shorter over the years, creeping up the thigh every season, but as late as 1904 the FA was still insisting that they should be long enough to cover the knees. This was abandoned after a year as most players preferred them shorter. They then became known as knickers – a word which still appeared in match programmes until the 1960s, when shorts took over.

J. BLAIR

K. CAMPBELL

ANDY CUNNINGHAM

SAM CHEDGZOY

G. WILSON

ABOVE Early players also played in caps, another of the public-school influences, but soon they became for ceremonial use only, awarded to international players.

RIGHT Stephen Smith of Aston Villa proudly wears his England international cap in 1895.

Early players also played in caps, often complete with tassels, another of the public-school influences. Some wore 'cowls', which were like floppy night caps or modern bobble hats. They must have been awkward to wear, especially when heading the ball, not that much heading was done in the early days. Caps had disappeared on the pitch by the time the professionals arrived, but were retained for ceremonial use, awarded to an international player, just as public-school boys were awarded their house colours or prefect caps.

The programme for a match between the Wanderers and Queen's Park held at Hampden Park in Glasgow, Queen's Park's ground, in October 1875, gives the colours of the caps the players were wearing, and the colour of their socks. This helped to identify each player as of course there were no numbers on the shirts. Most of the Wanderers, ex-public-school boys from London, were in caps, but only one of the Queen's Park players wore such headgear.

In the Wanderers side that day was the formidable A. F. Kinnaird as the right half-back while the captain is C. W. Alcock, Secretary of the FA. The line-up is interesting. Wanderers had three defenders and seven forwards, while Queen's Park had four defenders, three 'back-ups' and three forwards. There was still at this stage an umpire from either side (though it would appear Wanderers had not brought one from London, borrowing one from the Clydesdale Club), with a referee to adjudicate between them.

The one-sheet programme warns spectators: 'Please do not strain the ropes.' It must have been hard not to, with such a riot of clashing and dazzling colours and caps to gape at.

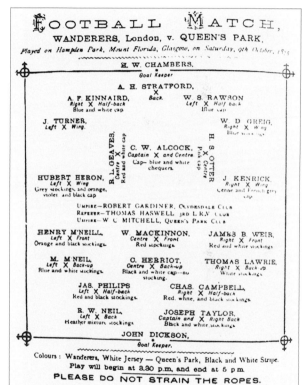

BELOW Wanderers-Queen's Park programme, 1875. Note the positions, caps, socks, but please do not strain the ropes!

WHEN BOOTS MEANT ... BOOTS

Ordinary boots or stout shoes were worn at first, but very soon special football boots were being made. The FA rules did not specify their style or shape, but from the beginning in 1863 they said there must be no projecting nails, possibly because the habit had already been established of players nailing bits of leather to their soles to give better purchase. They in turn became studs, which appeared as early as 1886, according to an advertisement in the July 31, 1886 issue of *Cricket and Football Field*, a publication based in Bolton. You could buy a gross of Ellis's Patent Boot Studs for six shillings, plus a tool for fixing at three pence. A letter from the Secretary of Kilmarnock FC assured readers they were 'a wonderful improvement in making football boots suitable for any weather'.

Boots were made of solid leather, came up over the ankle, with special patches on the ankles to add extra protection, and the toecaps were of such toughened leather they felt and weighed like pig iron. They naturally took some breaking in, when brand new.

PREVIOUS PAGE Bert Higgins, left, once Watford's goalkeeper, serves a customer at his gents outfitters in 1932. Many ex-footballers went on to open shops or run pubs.

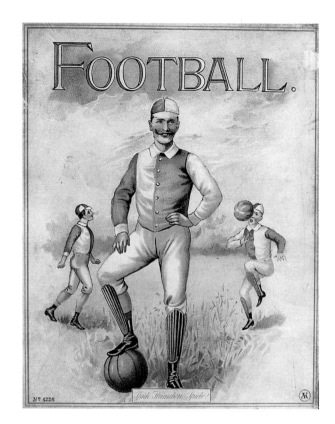

LEFT No footballer was complete without shinpads, worn over the socks at first and invented in 1874 by Sam Widdowson who played for Nottingham Forest. They were soon exported to all football playing countries, as seen on this German made toy-box from the 1890s.

In his 1937 book *Association Football* F. N. S Creek, a well-known Corinthian player, gives some jolly good advice about boots. 'If it is necessary to buy an inexpensive pair, a good tip is to fasten them correctly over the stockings and inners, then sit on the edge of the bath with the boots soaking in tepid water for about half an hour. This gives the cheap leather a chance to shrink or stretch. The boots are next allowed to dry slowly – NOT in front of the fire – and are finally well greased with dubbin.'

Mr Creek also offers a handy hint about lace-up shirts, still clearly very popular in 1937. 'Players, especially schoolboys, are often given out shirts which fasten at the neck with a lace which has half an inch of tin at the end for easy threading: this should be cut off at once as in the past it has proved dangerous when the lace flicks up into the player's face.' Ouch.

Early players often wore belts, some of them rather broad belts, corseted round the waist, like nineteenth-century boxers, presumably to support the muscles or keep in the stomach or just make you look tough and frighten the opposition. The Hearts players in a 1876 photo are all wearing belts, but quite neat ones. Perhaps in their case it was just to keep up their troosers.

Belts must have continued well into the twentieth century as a 1912 book, *Complete Association Footballer*, gave some handy advice about them. 'If a belt is worn, care should be taken that a buckle does not rest on the hip bone as in charging it will cause considerable pain to the wearer and his victim.'

Braces were sometimes worn as well, either under or over the jersey. When worn under the jersey, holes were cut in it to let the braces through, so that the jersey could still be tucked into the knickerbockers. No complete footballer was soon without shinpads, which were invented in 1874 by Sam Widdowson who played for Nottingham Forest – and later for England. They were worn over the socks at first, coming up as high as the bottom of the knickerbockers. By 1900, they had got smaller, neater and tucked inside the socks, as today. It's one of the ways in which you can date early photographs. Mr Creek in his 1937 book is all for shinpads. 'When I was a boy at school, it was considered effeminate to wear shin-guards for soccer. Thank goodness this idea has now largely disappeared. No shin-guard is going to prevent a broken leg, but the dozens of ordinary blows will be softened if some kind of protection is worn.' He gives a good tip for those unable to afford to buy their own shin guards. 'A piece of folded newspaper or cardboard is all that is required.'

THE SPORTSWEAR INDUSTRY IS BORN

What with all this paraphernalia required or available for manly chaps desirous of playing football, combined with the explosion in mass football in the 1880s and the hundreds of leagues and clubs that were starting up, a new industry had been created: manufacturing football equipment. The manufacturers in turn spawned wholesalers and retailers in every town in the land.

The earliest advertisements for football equipment that I have been able to find are from the 1880s, but manufacturers, as opposed to local cobblers producing one-off balls and hand-made boots for bespoke customers, probably started some time in the 1870s. By the 1900s, they are everywhere, in all sporting newspapers and annuals or magazines covering boys' interests.

Gamages, the London store in Holborn, took space in all the national prints for its vast range of footballs and other accessories which you could get mail order – carriage free for orders over 10 shillings. Their cheapest

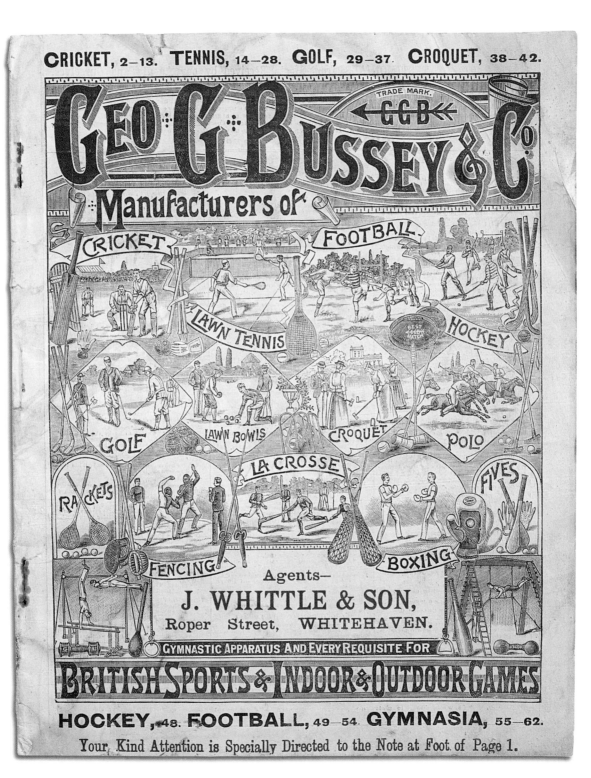

football in 1895, the Universal, with 'cowhide cases and rubber bladders', started at 3/3 while their top of the range was called the Referee, which cost 10/6. John Lewis department stores also offered a wide variety.

Manufacturers, national and local, liked to boast about their latest styles and systems. An Accrington firm called Riley's proclaimed that their Royal Wonder Football, price 6/6 was 'buttonless', while their Cup Tie Football, price 7/6, had 'button ends'. Buttons were presumably what they called the patched bit at the end. From around 1900, end patches started to disappear and all footballs were made up from interconnecting leather patches, like a jigsaw pattern, with no ends, no top or bottom, apart of course from the lace. In photographs of the time there often seems to be a bit of lace hanging out, but perhaps this was for carrying or holding the ball during photo opportunities.

Gamages would appear to have become about the biggest retailer of football equipment. In a 1906 advertisement, it said it was providing 'Everything for Football' and claimed to be the 'world's best and cheapest outfitters'. Its good were all English manufactured and in case you didn't quite get the patriotic message, it warned 'Beware of Foreign Rubbish!'

One of the bigger manufacturers of sports goods in the 1880s, judging by their beautifully produced, illustrated 60-page trade catalogue, was Geo G. Bussey of Peckham, London, who supplied shops and wholesalers all over the country. They were clearly at the top end of the market, making balls for Eton College. In their list of testimonials from satisfied customers they printed one from Mr William Elliot, professional to Winchester College. 'I bought your balls last season and I can say that I never had such balls before. I never had a damaged one.'

Mr Hughes, full-back for Cardiff FC, was stated to have 'kicked more goals from the GGB footballs than any others and considers them the most perfect for goal kicking he ever played with.' What was a full-back doing scoring so many goals? Sign him up.

There was a secret to Bussey's excellent balls, or so their catalogue suggested. 'Their superiority is largely due to the thorough knowledge gained by the late founder of the firm who was a well-known leather expert and whose experience of the old and undoubtedly more effective system of tanning with oak bark instead of chemicals which are now commonly used has enabled the present managers to select such rawhides of suitable tannage as are peculiarly suited to football requirements.'

OPPOSITE The front page of Geo Bussey's 60-page sports equipment catalogue from the 1880s. The firm was in Peckham, London, but supplied goods, and their catalogues, to shops and wholesalers as far north as Whitehaven.

Their best ball was the GGB Association Match Ball, which cost 12/6, but you could also get a Kaffir Ball at 6/6 and a Wonder Ball at 5/6. GGB also supplied bladders from 1/, football pumps from 1/6, shin-guards from 1/, plus football players' bags from 5/, to keep all your tackle in. In the 1880s they were still selling football belts, in various designs, from 4/ each.

Bussey's manufactured almost every form of football gear which required wood and leather in their own extensive workshops. From linesman's flags to ground markers. Their most expensive football item was a complete set of goals, with nets, for six guineas. A bargain.

One surprising thing in their 1880s catalogue was specialist goalkeeper's gloves from 5/, something I thought had not come in till more modern times. On the same page, they were selling Football Ear Guards, illustrated by a drawing of a moustachioed player wearing one, tied under his chin with a bow. They have not survived, but presumably they were very useful for centre forwards when charging into the goalie.

By 1900, factories and shops all over Britain were employing thousands of people making football equipment. In 1905, William Shillcock, a Birmingham manufacturer, wrote in an article that he believed the nation now depended on it. 'Don't let people talk about abolishing football or this country will suffer industrially as well as physically.' In other words, football was helping the health of the country in every sense.

Shillcock said he had 30 different styles of balls, including the McGregor, named after the founder of the League. In 1905, he was selling between forty thousand and fifty thousand balls a year. 'My own speciality is an improved chrome leather called "tufisto".'

It's interesting how manufacturers, then and now, love to go on about the scientific nature of their football products. But he also added one boast which even he must have realised one day might be contradicted. 'The football of today is as perfect as a football need be.'

Shillcock has another claim to football fame. In 1895, he had on display in his Birmingham showroom the FA Cup which had been won that year by Aston Villa – until on September 11 it was stolen from his shop window. The FA fined Villa £25, for having allowed it out of their hands, and had a replica cup made. The original one was never heard of again – until in 1958, a Sunday newspaper reported that Harry Burge, then aged 83, had confessed that he had stolen it, 63 years earlier, and had had it melted down into half crowns.

GEO. G. BUSSEY & CO., Manufacturers.

SHIN GUARDS.

LARGE SIZE. ℗ pair.

173 B   1st quality Leather ... 2/6
173 C   2nd   „   „   ... 2/-
173 D   3rd   „   „   ... 1/6
173 E   Strong Canvas   ... 1/-

SMALL SIZE.

173 H   Superior Leather   ... 1/6
173 K   Strong   „   ... 1/-
173 M   „   Canvas   ... -/9

LARGE SIZE. ℗ pair.

173 BA   1st quality Leather   ... 3/-
173 CA   2nd   „   „   ... 2/6
173 DA   3rd   „   „   ... 2/-
173 EA   Strong Canvas 1/6

SMALL SIZE.

173 HA   Superior Leather   ... 2/-
173 KA   Strong   „   ... 1/6
173 MA   „   Canvas   ... 1/-

GOAL KEEPERS' GLOVES.

173 GK White Leather, Red
   Rubber   ... per pair 5/9

173 HK Buff Leather, Black
   Rubber   ... per pair 5/-

FOOTBALL EAR GUARDS.

173 EG Gold Cape   ... 3/- each.
173 FG Chamois   ... 2/3 „
173 UG The "University Guard,"
   netted head   ... each 3/-

ANKLE GUARDS.

For the protection of the ankles
when ordinary boots are worn.

173 AG, 2/3 per pair.

FOOTBALL PLAYERS' BAGS.

Superior Cowhide,
371 C   14/6

Good Cowhide,
371 D   12/6

Waterproof Duck,
371 G   10/6

Waterproof Canvas,
371 K   8/6

G. G. BUSSEY & Co.

Roomy Shape, Size 16-inch.

THE "UNION" BAG.

Strong, Light,
Handy, Waterproof.

401 UB 5/- each.

FOOTBALL BELTS.

63 MS Web, 2 in., single strapped   ... 1/- each.

63 PS Web, 2 in., wide strap, new pattern ... 1/3 each.

63 OSR Web, 2½ in., double strapped   ... 1/3 each.

GGB

BUSSEY'S PATENT SPRING ATHLETIC BELT.

63 NP 1½ inch wide ... 3/- each.
63 OP 2   „   „   ...4/- „

WEB BELT.

63 T Regulation Spring Belt   ...   ... 8/- each.
63 Q Web Belt, 3 inches wide, 2 buckles 2/3 „
63 R   „   „   4   „   3   „   3/6 „
63 S   „   „   „   4   „   4/3 „

REGULATION SPRING BELT.

LAWS OF FOOTBALL.

64 KP, 2d. each. Orders must state whether "Association" or "Rugby" are required.

SPECIAL TERMS GIVEN TO CLUBS AND SCHOOLS FOR CASH.

LEFT Some of the equipment on offer for football players in the 1880s. The goalkeeper's gloves look surprisingly modern, but the Football Ear Guards are not used by footballers today, though they would come in handy in dressing rooms when a manager applies the hairdryer technique or kicks objects around.

Bring on the Players

4

WHAT WAS IT LIKE being a player in the early decades of professional football? Good fun is the first answer. Thousands of young working-class men, who could never have imagined earning a living by kicking a ball about, were very pleased. Far better than a dirty, grinding factory, plus a chance to see a bit of the world, or at least get down to London now and again. And it was quite well paid. Not in comparison with today, but compared with the sort of job they might otherwise have done.

In 1901, a maximum wage for professional players was established at £4 a week. Sounds piddling, but at the time the best-paid worker was getting no more than £2 a week. So roughly speaking, a professional footballer earned about twice as much as a skilled craftsmen or three times as much as an ordinary unskilled worker. It didn't set him up in luxury, far less for life, and was not enough to separate him from his roots and his previous lifestyle, but it did give him a few bob in his pocket for a few years.

In 1910, the maximum wage was £5 a week. By 1920 it had crept up to £9 a week, but two years later it dropped to £8 and remained at that level until the war, still around two to three times the average wage.

The reasoning behind a maximum wage was twofold. Firstly, prejudice. There was still among many FA officials and older football supporters a belief that football should be played for fun, not money, otherwise standards of behaviour would be lowered, ideals of sportsmanship ignored. Secondly, the FA and the Football League were worried about the richer clubs tempting away the best players, therefore becoming even richer and stronger, while the weak got weaker. It's a worry that persists to this day and one which no amount of legislation or lofty ideals seems able to eliminate. The problem remains.

OPPOSITE Billy Foulke, one of the best-known early football stars. He was six feet two and fifteen stone in 1894, aged nineteen, when he first appeared in goal for Sheffield United. After that, his career and his weight blossomed.

The 1901 thinking was that if the best players could earn no more than £4 a week, at any club, there would be little point in them moving around. Hence there should be equality. Fat chance, of course. There are always ways of tempting a player away, such as under-the-counter inducements and perks, not to mention a natural desire to move to a better club anyway, with better players and a better chance to win more pots.

The 1901 maximum wage rules also instituted the idea of benefits for players after every five years they remained at the same club, another reason, so it was presumed, for players to stay put. Players' wages went down marginally in the summer, but even so they were being paid for doing nothing, so most of the football public believed, and could also do other little jobs, which many did, even during the football season.

The Professional Footballers Union was formed in 1898 in Manchester, the early activists being Manchester United players, but the union was not recognised for another ten years by either the FA or the Football League. In 1908 they threatened strike action, then backed down when the FA agreed to acknowledge their existence.

There was a huge social and financial gap between professional players and directors, most of whom were well-off, local businessmen, determined to keep players in their place. Professional players did not appear in polite company or get introduced to ladies or people of quality. They stayed among the masses, recognised in pubs and offered free drinks, and often free seats for the local music hall, which might mean they got introduced on stage to loud cheers on a Saturday evening, if of course they had won.

THE LEGENDARY CORINTHIANS

Amateur players were a different breed socially. Until professionalism was legalised in 1885, most clubs and most players were amateurs, supposedly. Even afterwards there were many excellent amateurs playing for professional clubs, who often took their meals separately, and some very strong totally amateur clubs, notably the Corinthians, founded in 1882, who in 1886 supplied nine players to the England team. The Corinthians were all ex-public-school and Oxbridge players and their aim was to uphold the highest values of the amateur game, which meant they would not take part in any competitions or for prizes or ever argue with the referee. If a player on the other side got sent off or had to leave through injury, they were known to voluntarily play with ten men, to keep it fair.

But they were an excellent team, right up to the First World War, capable of defeating most of the big professional clubs. In 1904, they beat the FA Cup winners Bury 10–3. They liked to think that their amateur values helped make them so good. In the *Annals of the Corinthian Football Club* published in 1906, B. O. Corbett scorned the professional game as based on 'mechanical activity and laborious training', unlike the amateur who relied on natural instinct. 'The amateur is essentially independent and it is this individualism, combined with his public-school training, which makes his style of play so distinctive.'

BELOW The legendary Corinthians who were founded in 1882 travelled widely playing in matches as far away as South Africa.

ABOVE Blackburn Rovers in 1905 in their distinctive halved shirts but in an unusual line-up in the goalmouth before a match.

The Corinthians were one of the earliest British clubs to go on foreign tours, taking football to the 'natives' and also having a good time. On a voyage to South Africa in 1897, despite running into a terrible storm, they all managed to turn out for a fancy-dress ball. 'In which every one of the team took part, some of the dresses being excellent, in spite of the limited facilities for making them on board.' In South Africa, when not playing games, there were endless banquets, picnics and shooting parties.

On a Hungarian tour in 1904, there was some trouble with the Austrian customs who made them open up their luggage, during which officials unearthed a large number of cigars and in the process, oh horrors, 'left the greasy prints of their fingers on some dress shirts'.

During their tour of the USA and Canada in 1906, one of the players, an ex-Oxford man, was alarmed to come down to breakfast in a hotel in Toronto and find a note by his plate: 'You are requested to see the Dean at ten o'clock.' It was a trick played by one of the waiters, who some years previously had been his college scout. 'He was so pleased to see his old master again that he took it for granted his presumption would be overlooked.'

They were very tough, the Corinthians, never complaining when roughed up, taking it like men. Corbett tells a tale of one player, E. C. Bambridge, known as Bam, whose 'pluck was proverbial', who had been out with a broken limb but was determined to play in a vital match although the bone had not yet mended. He arrived wearing one large white shin-guard outside his stocking which by half-time was covered in blood where the opposition had been kicking him. He refused to be intimidated, and in the second half scored the winning goal. In the dressing room afterwards, he took off his shin-guard and revealed he had put it on his sound limb. 'The injured one had been unprotected – and untouched.'

Looking at the photos of the amateur teams in the early years, you see a certain swagger and swank as they stand in their pristine jerseys and knickerbockers, trying hard to be individuals, striking personal poses, some lounging at the front, others sitting sideways. The captain was usually very easy to spot, looking captain-like, aloof from the team.

No photograph exists of the very first international match in 1872 between Scotland and England, because none of the players would promise to buy prints from the photographer. How mean of them, considering they were well-bred, ex-public-school amateurs. With the coming of the professionals, a uniform, regimental team photograph soon took over. There was a period when some teams lined up in the goalmouth for their team shot, in a straight line, but this didn't last long, and from about 1905 onwards the standard team photo was established, with two rows of players with the captain in the middle of the front row, holding the ball. It continues to this day. You see players automatically grouping themselves, without being asked, having seen photographs of football teams in the same formation.

Professional players, just as today, were quick to copy each other's hairstyles, following the fashions among smart young men of their time. Middle partings and moustaches were very popular in the 1920s, as shaved heads are today.

Players were always interested in clothes, judging by a paragraph in the Chelsea programme from 1907. 'A display of caps in shop windows exercises the same fascination over football players as the milliner's latest styles do over their sisters, cousins and wives.' Chelsea were and are based in a fashionable district and have always attracted fashionable players.

In that same programme there is a witty reference to the latest styles on the pitch, with players starting to wear shorter shorts. In describing one

WILLS'S CIGARETTES

R. W. WESTWOOD *BOLTON WANDERERS.*

WILLS'S CIGARETTES

L. J. JONES *(COVENTRY CITY)*

WILLS'S CIGARETTES

E. DRAKE *(ARSENAL)*

WILLS'S CIGARETTES

W. FURNESS *(LEEDS UNITED)*

ABOVE Professional players, just as today, were quick to copy each other's hairstyles, following the fashions among smart young men of their time.

player showing a lot of naked flesh, they said 'it was about a shilling cab fare from the top of his stockings to the nearest portion of his nether garments'.

PROFESSIONALS IN TRAINING

There is a feeling in football, among players and fans, that they didn't train in the olden days, didn't care about their health and diet, not like today. The gentlemen amateurs of course just turned up. During the day, they were otherwise engaged anyway, in the City, in their chambers, on their country estates. But the moment professionalism arrived, the top teams did take training quite seriously.

Before the FA Cup Final of 1883, between Old Etonians and Blackburn Olympic (not to be confused with Blackburn Rovers),Olympic went off to a health hydro near Blackpool for a week's preparation. Their diet consisted of a glass of port wine at six in the morning, followed by two raw eggs and a walk along the sands. For breakfast they had porridge and haddock. Lunch was a leg of mutton. Tea was more porridge and a pint of milk. Supper was a dozen oysters each. It seemed to work. In the final they beat the Old Etonians 2–1, becoming the first non-public-school team to win the FA Cup.

By 1905, professional clubs like Aston Villa and West Brom, Woolwich Arsenal and Spurs, had a gymn on the premises, communal baths and a trainer who gave massages and rub-downs.

In an issue of *CB Fry's Magazine* of 1904, a publication devoted to all sports, one of the writers goes along to Spurs at White Hart Lane and watches them in training. (Very much as I did in writing *The Glory Game* in 1972. I thought, at the time, I was the first to write about Spurs from the inside – little knowing I'd been beaten to it almost 70 years earlier ...)

The article is entitled 'Spurs in Mufti' and contains photographs of the players in their dressing room with, in the middle, a half-naked player having treatment. The Spurs trainer was Sam Mountford. 'Sammy expects them to put in an appearance at the ground soon after ten in the morning. They have an hour to an hour and half sprinting and ball practice, with turns at skipping, which is excellent exercise for the muscles of the feet and legs. A bath and a rub-down complete the morning's work.'

Before a cup-tie, they went into much stricter training, which lasted all day and included lots of long walks. Sammy did not ban smoking or drinking. 'If a man wants to drink or smoke, no prohibition will prevent him.' He was a great believer in a lot to eat, the more varied the better. 'They are never allowed to tire of any new dish.'

In charge of the team was the player-manager John Cameron, a tough-sounding Scotsman, only 32 years old. 'Mr Cameron regards the left half-back as the most difficult place on the field to find a man for, though centre forward runs it pretty close.' Spurs had a training ground at Chingford at which there was a stuffed squirrel in a case, caught while the team was training. At White Hart Lane, next to the stadium, was the players' social club. 'Here, the comforts of a home are provided and the men may read, write, play billiards or cards, as fancy takes them. Needless to say, the club is greatly appreciated.' I should say. In 1972, the players had no such facilities.

The article doesn't mention any work on tactics but tactics did exist, ever since Scotland introduced the passing game. From the 1880s onwards, the formation had settled down to 2–3–5 with two full-backs, three half-backs and five forwards, which was how it remained for almost the next 100 years, as can be seen in any printed programme, though internally the functions were not always as formalised. In the early decades, the centre half was seen as a creative player, coming forward all the time, but in 1925, when the offside law was changed from three to two opposing players, the centre half then stayed back, usually to mark the centre forward.

The amateur view that football was meant to be fun and instinctive made it hard for the early coaches and trainers to get their ideas across. 'It is a common thing to hear men say that training for football is a foolish fad,' so wrote J. L. Jones, captain of Spurs, in his 1904 book, *Association Football*.

He devoted a whole chapter to training, pointing out how tired forwards have lost many a game, being unable to repeat the energy of the first half. So keeping fit was vital, lots of walks and running and exercises. 'I am not an enthusiast over dumb-bells but club-swinging may be practised with advantage.' On the whole, he thought the ordinary average working man's diet was fine. 'As wholesome as it is nourishing. Very few alterations need be made.' He approved of eggs, toast, a steak or chops for breakfast, roast beef or boiled mutton for dinner, but was not keen on pork, bacon or venison, which he believed upset the stomach. As for drinking, he would not allow spirits but 'beer is so much a recognised article of diet that it would be impossible, or at least unwise, to forbid it.' He was all against smoking, though, but admitted that getting regular smokers to give up was difficult. 'As for the smoking of cigarettes by boys and young men, I cannot find words strong enough to express my disapproval. The habit of smoking once started may lead to grave disasters. Lungs and nerves at least are permanently affected.' Strong words, for 1904.

While in training, and at half-times in matches, he personally favoured one drink in particular. 'Oxo is very nourishing and refreshing.' I'm sure he meant it sincerely, but at the end of his book was a whole page advert for, wait for it, Oxo. Could this be one of the first examples of product placement? The advert boasted that Manchester City, winners of the 1904 FA Cup, had trained on Oxo during the whole season.

Billy Bassett, one of the stars of the 1890s, who played 16 seasons for West Brom and was capped 16 times for England, was of the opinion that modern training was being overdone. In 1905, by which time he was a director of West Brom, he wrote that the 'man plays football best who works for his living in the ordinary way'. On the other hand, he could not criticise footballers who were fortunate enough to be on £4 a week who had given up work completely, so some sort of training was probably quite good for them. 'Time hangs heavily on the paid footballer's hands.'

In Billy Bassett's day, he was lucky to have a bucket of cold water after a game, now clubs had hot baths and proper gymnasiums. Clearly they were getting soft. He also thought they were sometimes not as smart as they should be. 'I do not like to see footballers getting £4 per week for slouching about in mufflers.'

Like almost all ex-footballers throughout the ages, he had fond memories of his day. 'There used to be a lot of wild doings, and they make

The English Cup.

The Players of the

MANCHESTER CITY FOOTBALL CLUB,

Winners of the English Association Football Cup, 1904, trained on OXO during the whole Season.

The following letter speaks for itself:—

Manchester, 7th April, 1904.

"I have much pleasure in testifying to the sustaining properties of OXO, the 'City' team having used it regularly during the Season."

(signed) THOS. E. MALEY, Secretary and Manager, MANCHESTER CITY FOOTBALL CLUB.

"Got It."

OXO

ABOVE Billy Foulke in 1904, by then known universally as 'Fatty Foulke', having grown to 22 stone while keeping goal for Chelsea. Later, at Bradford City, he was 25 stone.

very interesting reminiscences. I don't suppose footballers of the future will ever have such riotous fun as their predecessors had.' Hmm, I wouldn't be too sure of that.

He quotes Mr McGregor – founder of the Football League and still then at Aston Villa – as recommending that golf would be a good form of exercise for footballers, but he points out one problem. 'Golf clubs are generally somewhat exclusive. If all the professional footballers in a team were to make an application for a club, I do not think they would get in.'

THE FETED AND THE FAT

The first football heroes were the amateurs, like Kinnaird and Alcock and G. O. Smith of Oxford and the Corinthians, their names becoming known to all football fans of the time. Vivian Woodward of Spurs, one of the last amateur stars to play in a professional team, became famous when he scored six goals for England against Holland in 1909. But it was the professional players who quickly became household names, in football households, such as John Goodall, inside forward for the Preston North End 'Invincibles' team of 1889. Forwards, like Billy Bassett, tended to become the stars, as they do today, attracting all the headlines, acclaimed as 'Wizards of Dribble'. Steve Bloomer of Derby was famous as a prolific goalscorer, scoring 353 league goals between 1892 and 1914. As early as 1892, one commentator, C. Edwards, was writing that star players were becoming 'better known than the local member of Parliament'.

One of the earliest, most recognisable stars was in fact a goalkeeper – Billy Foulke. He was 6ft 2ins high and weighed 15 stone at the age of 19 when he first played for Sheffield United in 1894, later reaching 22 stone, but this didn't stop him helping United win the league championship and the cup twice and getting an England cap. In the days when goalies could still be charged into the net, his weight was clearly an advantage.

'Fatty' Foulke then moved to Chelsea where he was made captain and adored by the fans. 'I don't mind what they call me as long as they don't call me late for my lunch.' At Chelsea, he was known to arrive early for breakfast, set for the entire Chelsea team, and scoff the lot. On the pitch, he once grabbed a forward who had annoyed him and dangled him upside down in the muddy goalmouth. But he was still reckoned an excellent goalie.

'Perhaps the most talked of player in the world – a leviathan at 22 stone with the agility of a bantam,' so Foulke was described in 1904 in *The Men*

Who Made Football. 'The cheeriest of companions, brims over with good humour. His ponderous girth brings no inconvenience and the manner in which he gets down to low shots explodes any idea that a superfluity of flesh is a handicap. At Chelsea, he has amused the crowd by punching the ball from his goal to well over the halfway line! Scorns to pick the ball up with both hands.'

Foulke ended his playing career with Bradford City, by which time he was said to be 25 stone. He cashed in on his fame after his retirement by appearing on Blackpool beach, saving penalties for pennies, but it was there in 1916, aged only 42, that he caught a chill and died.

Fatty Foulke was a legend in his time, but probably the best remembered from that pre-First World War period, in the sense that he still appears in all the record books, is Alf Common. What a sensation he created in February 1905 when he was transferred from Sunderland to Middlesbrough for the then astronomical sum of £1,000, the first ever four-figure transfer fee.

The FA and the League, having imposed a maximum wage, had contemplated a maximum transfer fee, and in 1899 the FA suggested the limit should be £10, but they felt unable to impose it, so over the next few years it slowly crept up to around £400 for the best players. A sudden jump to £1,000 amazed everyone. An investigation was set up to find out if anything unlawful had been done. The transfer was all above board, but when they went through the Boro books, it was revealed they'd paid illegal cup bonuses to players in the previous season.

Football purists were aghast, saying it was the end of football as they had known it. Money was ruining the game, players had become mercenaries with no loyalties, a new form of white slave trade had now been introduced, where will it end – will we soon have £2,000 transfers or even, perish the thought, will there one of these days be a £10,000 transfer fee?

Part of the surprise was the fact that it was Middlesbrough, a relatively new club, only six years old. But Boro that season were desperate, struggling near the bottom of the First Division and badly in need of a goalscorer. Some things never change. They had tried for one, who turned them down, and so decided to lash out on Sunderland's bustling, 5ft-8ins-high, 13-stone Alf Common.

Sunderland had bought him from Sheffield United just a year previously for £350, so naturally Sheffield United were pretty livid that Sunderland had made such a huge profit in a short time. Charles Clegg, chairman of the FA, who was also a Sheffield United man, was particularly upset.

As so often happens in football, with almost predictable irony, Common's first game for Boro, on February 25, 1905, was away to Sheffield United. They won 1–0, with Common scoring from a penalty. It was Boro's first away win for nearly two years and they stayed up, with Common taking over as captain. So, this first ever shock-horror mega transfer deal was considered money well spent.

Common was a jovial, ruddy-faced, rather tubby player, famous for his attempts to lose weight. Sounds like another well-known North-Easterner, P. Gascoigne. At the age of 30, Common was transferred to Woolwich Arsenal who devised all sorts of physical exercises and strenuous walks to get him slim, without much success. When he retired he became a publican, running the Alma Hotel at Cockerton for 11 years. 'A footballer behind the bar is as great an attraction as a long-legged giant or a fat woman,' reported the *Athletic Journal* as early as 1890.

The tradition of players becoming publicans lived on for almost the next 100 years, at least for those who had managed to save a few pounds. Even as late as 1974, it was what Sir Alex Ferguson first did when his career with Rangers and Ayr United was coming to an end. At the time, he wasn't quite sure what to do with the rest of his life.

Alf Common was known as a practical joker, but alas none of his wheezes have survived. Footballers have always been known for their amusing as well as riotous behaviour, as Billy Basset indicated.

A writer in the *Book of Football* in 1905 described one of the tricks which the Newcastle United players got up to while travelling by train. They had a special saloon provided by the North Eastern Railway Company, divided into two compartments by a sliding door, where the players passed the time playing whist. If a bossy ticket collector interrupted their games by laboriously checking the tickets and counting all the players, they deliberately set out to confuse him. When the ticket inspector announced that there were 22 players, yet only 16 tickets, he naturally suspected some fiddle was going on, and he proceeded to call for the station master. Only later did he discover that some players had been sliding between the two doors and had been counted twice. What japes.

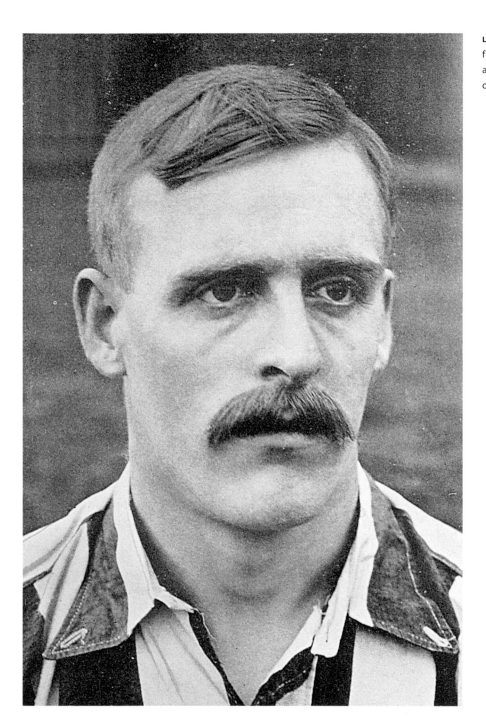

LEFT Alf Common, the world's first transfer. He was known as a practical joke, but alas none of his wheezes have survived.

Supporting Football: The History of Spectators

5

THE 1901 FA CUP FINAL was between Tottenham Hotspur and Sheffield United and held at the Crystal Palace in London. Spurs at the time were still in the Southern League, so that was a remarkable achievement, but what was phenomenal was how many spectators turned up: 114,815, the largest gathering which had ever attended a football match. Yet football as a professional sport was only 15 years old. Who were they? Where had they come from? What did they all do?

A lot of eating for a start, as spectators still do today. During that game, the supporters consumed 120,000 slices of bread and butter, 100,000 Bath Buns, 6,000 pork pies, 1,778 gallons of milk, 200 rumps of beef, 40 whole lambs, 500lbs of sole. They drank 120,000 bottles of mineral water and copious amounts of tea, coffee and alcohol. A good time was clearly had by all, as the game ended in a 2–2 draw. (Spurs went on to win the replay 3–2.)

Crowds at ordinary league grounds in the first part of the twentieth century were often enormous, especially in the 1920s and 1930s, setting ground records which in many cases have not been broken since. Manchester City drew 84,000 for a game against Stoke City in 1934. Chelsea drew 83,000 in 1935 for a game against Arsenal. Arsenal got 73,000 for a game against Sunderland in 1935. Aston Villa drew 74,000 in 1930 against Walsall (that was in the cup). Bolton Wanderers had 69,000 in 1933 against Manchester City. Charlton in 1938 had 76,000 against Villa. Sunderland had 75,000 against Derby in 1933. Spurs had 75,000 against Sunderland in 1938. Sheffield Wednesday had 73,000 against Manchester City in 1934. Sheffield United got 68,000 against Leeds United in 1936. Newcastle had 68,000 in 1930 against Chelsea. West Brom had 65,000 against Arsenal in 1937. Wolves had 61,000 against Arsenal in 1938.

OPPOSITE Tony Adams of Arsenal was often described as a donkey by rival fans, which of course was very unfair, but donkeys in football have a long history among supporters. Who can forget Amos, official mascot of Barnsley Football Club. In 1910, as this photograph proves, Barnsley also had their own national telephone number. Dial 320. If you heard hee haw, hee haw, hee haw, you knew who was answering. Supporters just like to have fun.

Blackburn Rovers had 62,000 against Bolton in 1929. Everton in 1938 got
68,000 against Sunderland. Huddersfield Town had 67,000 in 1932 for a
game against Arsenal. In Scotland, Celtic and Rangers regularly had crowds
of 90,000 for big games.

NORTHERN INVADERS

In England, the FA Cup Final always drew the biggest crowd each year,
especially after it moved to Wembley in 1923. That year there were officially
123,000 to see Bolton beat West Ham, but so many forced their way in it
was estimated the total might have been nearer 200,000.

That was a classic North-South confrontation, as it had been in 1901,
which always drew huge crowds and attracted great national interest. And
also reactions of shock-horror from the more refined members of London
society who were appalled by the sudden invasion of 'northern hordes of
uncouth garb and strange oaths' as they were described as early as 1884 by
an unnamed writer in the *Pall Mall Gazette*.

The London cab drivers welcomed the extra custom, but they were
mocking as well. In his memories of football games of the 1880s, *Wickets
and Goals*, 1926, J. A. H. Catton, describes what the old horse-drawn

omnibus drivers thought about the provincials in their club colours, up for the Final. They laughed and joked about the football folk, and twitted them. They called them 'lunies' and 'lunatics' and inquired, 'Does yer mother know ye're out?'

The regularity of northern invasions, double the size of course when two northern teams met in the Final, as happened in 1911 with Newcastle United playing Bradford City, continued to upset sensitive souls. In *The Graphic* of April 29, 1911, Philip Gibbs, under the headline 'The Barbarity of Cup Day', really let himself go.

'A horde of northern barbarians invaded London on Saturday, strolling in their big boots up Bond Street, staring under the peaks of their cloth caps, giving an unintelligent glance or two ... many with big fists and brawny shoulders, slouched along in their ready made suits ... hard and dour in the mould of their faces, not softness, nor grace nor elegance. London was a strange unknown to them and like sheer savages, they went stupidly about.

'There was a general rendezvous in the evening when the whole vast horde surged together into the heart of London, filled the music halls and picture theatres and, in an atmosphere of rank smoke and whisky fumes and

beer dregs, guffawed at the red-nosed comedians on stage, yawned at the dancing, slept in a fuddled way when the orchestra played soft music.

'It is rather awful to think that these loafers who invaded London have become decadent before becoming civilised. "What Lancashire thinks today England thinks tomorrow." Heaven help England if it is waiting upon the thoughts of the men whose hoarse voices roared at the Crystal Palace when a bladder ball was kicked to and fro about a field.'

Some good vituperative, class prejudice but not quite so hot on geography if he thought Newcastle and Bradford were in Lancashire.

CLUB COLOURS

Derby games also attracted large crowds with long processions of brakes – horse-driven coaches packed with up to 24 supporters each – all from the same area who would join together in a 'brake club', hiring transport for the day's outing, with ample beer for the journey.

From the 1890s onwards, as contemporary descriptions show, fans sported their club colours, decorating their coaches and themselves with banners and balloons. From about 1900, judging by photographs, they were wearing rosettes and waving rattles. A history of wooden rattles is long overdue, but they would appear to have been of rural origin, used to frighten away birds in the fields and later in factories to mark the end of shifts or attract attention, and then got taken to matches as excellent makers of noise.

For the big occasions, fans also put on silly hats, carried fancy umbrellas, waved and cheered and sang when walking in groups through the streets of London, and whenever they saw a camera pulled funny faces and hammed it up. What we see at World Cups today, with people dressing up in fancy clothes and painting their faces to support their country, was with us 100 years ago. Only the replica shirts are a modern creation. This habit of football fans turning big games into jolly, social events was never seen on the same scale at cricket grounds. It was often the only chance factory workers had to let off steam, and probably the only time in their lives they would visit the capital, purely to cheer on their team.

OPPOSITE An aerial view of the first FA Cup Final held at Wembley in 1923. Some 123,000 fans were officially there, but it's estimated that nearer 200,000 managed to get in, many of them spilling over onto the pitch.

BELOW Everton supporter in Trafalgar Square celebrates their 3–0 victory over Manchester City in the 1933 FA Cup Final.

What's interesting about these huge crowds, despite being labelled as savages by the society magazines, was their generally peaceful behaviour, though sometimes they did terrify ordinary locals, such as an observer who had been to a game at Shrewsbury in 1899. 'There were many thousands at Shrewsbury on Easter Monday and the concomitants of betting, drinking and bad language were fearful to contemplate while the shouting and horseplay on the highways were a terror to peaceful residents passing homewards.'

And yet for the first 80 or so years of organised football there was surprisingly little real trouble when you consider the vast numbers being shoved into primitive, dangerous and unhealthy conditions. Police figures and FA reports indicate very few serious football-related fighting incidents up until the 1970s. Crowds did boo the opposition, shout obscenities at referees, but they didn't thump each other and were generally law abiding.

TROUBLE ON THE TERRACES

The first known evidence of crowd trouble occurred in 1908 at Hampden Park at the Scottish Cup Final replay between Rangers and Celtic. It ended in a draw and the crowd had been expecting there would now be extra time. When they learned there was to be yet another game, they invaded the pitch, pulled down the goals and set fire to the pay boxes. Their action was directed not against each other but the Scottish FA, whom they suspected of trying to make more money by not having extra time. No one was killed, but many were injured.

There was only one notable football disaster during the period up to the Second World War. This was at Ibrox in 1902 for the Scotland v England game. Wooden planks in one of the stands gave way as the crowd swayed to get a better view. They collapsed and people fell through the gaps, resulting in 26 dead and 500 injured. Astonishingly, play continued to avoid further panic and many in the ground did not know there had been a disaster till they read about it in the papers next day.

The next major disaster did not occur for over another 40 years – in 1946 when 33 were killed at Burden Park, Bolton, during a cup game between Wanderers and Stoke watched by 65,000. Overcrowding on the terraces was to blame, with crush barriers collapsing. In modern times there have been far worse disasters, and yet the crowds have never reached the level of those pre-war years.

ABOVE The Ibrox disaster of 1902 during a Scotland-England game resulted in 26 dead and 500 injured when wooden planking collapsed. Many at the match did not know of the tragedy till they read about it in the papers next day.

The first football grounds were primitive affairs, little more than a field with a hut or perhaps a little pavilion for the quality to sit and watch while most spectators gathered behind ropes. You can see in early photographs of Cup Finals FA at the Oval and at Crystal Palace that most spectators were just standing in the open.

Modern stadia came in during the 1900s, spreading to all the major league clubs, and included huge, tiered stands and massive embankments created by earth-moving machinery. The mass of supporters stood on these terraces, held in by crush barriers. Some of these terraces were in theory protected from the rain by a jutting-out roof, so clubs could boast, as Spurs did in all its programmes in the 1920s, that there was 'Room for 40,000 Under Cover', which increased to 'Room for 60,00 Under Cover' in the 1930s – but in effect they were still open to the elements. No wonder so many hot pies and Bovril were sold and clothes manufacturers pushed mufflers and coats for football fans.

The 1902 Ibrox disaster came at a time when the stadium had recently been rebuilt and was meant to be the most modern in Britain. It was designed by the architect looked upon as the first to specialise in football stadia, a Scotsman called Archibald Leitch. He built Hampden Park and went on, despite the Ibrox disaster, to work on Hillsborough, Stamford Bridge, Craven Cottage and Ayresome Park, among others.

FLOODLIGHTS, SCOREBOARDS AND OTHER GIZMOS

The first floodlights were tried as early as 1878 for a demonstration game at Sheffield United's ground, Bramall Lane. A generator was installed at either end of the ground and lights hung from 30-feet-high wooden towers at the four corners. Nearly twenty thousand turned up and the promoters considered it had been a successful experiment. Three weeks later they were tried in London, for a game between Wanderers and Clapham Rovers, but the *Illustrated Sport and Country* was not impressed. 'Who wants to play football by artificial light? As a novelty, now and then, to attract wandering shillings, it may be all very well, but for the real purpose of the game, day light is quite good enough and long enough.'

Over the next few years, there were various other experiments, sometimes using flares instead of electricity. In Lancashire in the 1890s, an evening game was played with a spotlight following the ball around, which was painted white to help recognition, but spectators complained they

couldn't see it. In 1892, Celtic strung lights across the pitch 50 feet above it, but it was not a success as the ball kept on hitting the wires. The FA and the Football League were never keen, wanting to restrict games to Saturday afternoons, and in 1930 the FA officially banned clubs from taking part in floodlit games. Official sanction did not come till the 1950s.

Facilities and amenities at all grounds were limited, apart from the food and drink stalls, but from the early days, there was usually a band playing before and after the game, and often at half-time, marching up and down, either the town's local brass band or in the case of Arsenal, a police band, which could be seen at Highbury until the 1970s.

One of the early features at all league grounds, never seen in this age of audio and visual delights, was a manual system of telling you the half-time scores at other games, which of course true fans have always wanted to know. Large letters of the alphabet were hung in prominent places and the code would be printed in the programme, telling you that A represented Manchester United v Arsenal, B was Newcastle v Spurs.

During the game, old men and small boys could be spotted hanging numbers under them, telling you the scores. The system dates from the 1900s, and at some grounds the information system was so well organised, with telegraph and then telephone messages coming in from around the country, that the scores would be updated every 15 minutes.

While waiting for the latest scores, crowds could always amuse themselves by singing. One of the earliest known football songs was 'On the Ball City' which was sung by Norwich City fans as early as 1902. Often well- known songs of the day were taken over by fans, such as 'I love a Lassie', a song made famous by Harry Lauder, which was heard at both Bradford City and Nottingham Forest in 1911. Hymns were also popular. 'Abide with Me' was first sung at Wembley in 1927.

Rangers and Celtic fans were singing songs with sectarian overtones from the 1920s. Newcastle fans have been singing 'Blaydon Races' since at least the 1930s. Portsmouth's 'Pompey Chimes' dates from around the same time. West Ham fans are still singing 'I'm Forever Blowing Bubbles', and according to one folk legend it was first sung at the 1923 Wembley Cup Final, which is hardly likely, as the song, written by an American, didn't reach England until 1926. It really started in the 1930s when a London crowd noticed that a young player called Murray had a head of curly hair, which reminded them of a current advertisement for Pear's soap, a famous

one featuring a painting by Millais, of a boy blowing bubbles which in turn got them singing the bubbles song.

The very first spectators, watching the leading amateur sides composed of public-school boys, were mainly from the same class, cheering on the chaps. When the professional clubs took over, the fans became predominantly young working-class men. There was always a small proportion of women, who can be spotted in early crowd photographs if you peer hard, while in the grandstands, in the best seats, were some middle- class supporters, but the rough male culture of swearing and drinking, meant that many 'respectable' people would never have considered attending a football match.

The influence and interest of the amateur, public school football lovers, both as player and spectators, declined sharply after the First World War. Not simply because of the dominance of the big, northern professional clubs but because at the outbreak of war in 1914 the football authorities did not at once cancel all football fixtures, which many people considered disgusting and unpatriotic. After the war, many well-known schools who had played association football turned to rugby instead. From then on, watching football became primarily a working-class activity.

ABOVE There was always a small number of women in football crowds, who can be sported in old photos if you peer carefully enough. One appears to be the total among these West Ham fans at an FA Cup Semi-Final against Everton in 1933 – greatly outnumbered by men in silly hats, rosettes, pretend hammers and beer bottles, most of them empty. West Ham lost 1–2.

Writing about Football

6

OLD BOYS had their sporting interests and activities recorded in old boys' magazines, which mainly meant country pursuits like hunting, fishing, shooting and horseracing. In the mid-nineteenth century, when organised games flourished in the public schools, such as cricket, rugby and football, these were also included in the sporting prints. It was of course the introduction of professionalism that created a brand-new form of human activity – the football reporter.

In the late 1880s, there were three daily sporting newspapers – *The Sporting Chronicle*, *The Sporting Life* and *The Sportsman*, all of which concentrated on horseracing, offering betting intelligence. Very slowly, each of them began to cover football as well, though in a very minor way at first.

When in 1870 Charles Alcock of the FA first had his idea for an international between English and Scottish London-based teams, and was looking for likely players, he wrote to *The Sportsman* newspaper, asking for names to be submitted. Some of the early FA meetings were held at *The Sportsman*'s offices, and many of the early FA officials, including Alcock, wrote for *The Sportsman* and other publications.

The beginning of the Football League in 1888 meant not only regular games for players and fans, but also regular work for football writers. I have in my collection a run of *Sporting Chronicles* from July 3 to December 29, 1888 in other words, the first half of the first ever football season. The pages have dried out, like rice paper, and are in danger of falling to pieces, but they make fascinating reading.

At first it is hard to find any mention of football, as it is all racing, and of course still summer, but on August 16 all the league fixtures for Preston North End, Everton and Bolton were printed, then on September 8 the first

OPPOSITE A London *Evening Standard* newspaper seller in 1936. London had three evening papers at one time – the *Star*, *News* and *Standard* – who competed to be first on the streets on a Saturday evening with the football results. Every major city had Pink 'Uns or Green 'Uns, football editions produced at incredible speed, often printed in time for supporters still on their way home from the game.

OPPOSITE On November 19, 1888, the first season of the Football League, the *Sporting Chronicle* reported a 'Disgraceful Scene' at the Notts County v Everton game. One player struck another player in the back 'in a piece of ruffianism' and supporters were heard to shout 'Dog' and 'Pig'. Thank goodness nothing unseemly ever happens at football games today ...

matches took place. They were not all reported at first, and friendly games were still being played, some of them considered more important, such as Preston North End versus Glasgow on September 13, which attracted a crowd of fifteen thousand.

On October 19, the paper said that 'the League system has taken a firm root', despite a report of the Burnley v Everton game where 'a start was made at ten minutes past four before a large company'. On November 13, blows were exchanged at the match between Stoke and Preston North End. The Notts County game against Everton had the headline 'Disgraceful Scene'. The Nottingham crowd had turned against some Everton players, especially one called Dick. 'Epithets such as Dog! Pig! Were frequently bestowed on the visitors.' When the game ended, some spectators invaded the pitch and attacked the Everton players with sticks. 'Our correspondent adds that Dick played anything but a gentlemanly game, while his language was coarse, but even these defects did not merit mob law ...'

In these early reports, the ball was usually referred to as the 'leather', a goalkeeper was praised for being a 'good fister' and a forward for being good at 'screw kicks'. Over ten thousand turned up on December 27 to see West Brom against Preston North End, which sounds like the biggest crowd so far, despite the 'shooting being wretched'.

The Football League meeting at which they decided to award two points for a win and one for a draw is reported on November 22 – but they voted against a league for second teams. That same issue reports an FA commission on 'rough play'.

During these six months of *The Sporting Chronicle*, there are regular reports of the Canadian association football team who were on tour in Britain, which surprised me, indicating how quickly football must have been exported to Canada. There is also an account of a floodlit rugby game at Stockport which attracted a crowd of four or five thousand, using lights provided by the Manchester Ship Canal. They worked quite well, except the centre of the pitch was always in darkness.

On December 29, there was a report of what might well have been one of the first ever deaths at a football match. A 12-year-old boy, Thomas Coyle of Bradford, was killed while watching the Manningham Club play on Christmas Day. The coroner's inquest suggested the boy was partly to blame – he should have been in the boys' enclosure, but had trespassed on to the field of play. 'At an exciting point of the match' a sudden rush of spectators had caused the crush barriers to collapse and they had spilled on to the pitch, on top of the poor boy. As compensation his parents were to receive all the proceeds from the match, which came to £115.

The three main sporting dailies were nationals, but very quickly local papers started following the fortunes of their local clubs when they found that coverage of football sold papers. Football clubs realised that the right sort of publicity was good for them, if of course it showed them in a good light, and helped to bring in more supporters.

PIONEERING PAPERS

The weekly newspaper *Athletic News*, which had begun in Manchester in 1875, covering all amateur sports, began to cover football from around 1883 when its sales were twenty-five thousand. Ten years later, sales had increased fourfold as the paper gave more and more space to football. It was published on a Monday and contained reports of every league game. By 1919, its sales were 170,000 and it had become the leading football newspaper.

Its editor H. A. H. Catton, whose match reports under the name of 'Tityrus' were famous in their day, recalled in his memoirs, *Wickets and Goals*, his early years of football reporting, which began in 1875 when he joined the *Preston Herald* as a cub reporter. 'Up and down the touchline, exposed to the weather, the reporter had to wander like a restless spirit.' The only facilities, if he was lucky, was a wooden bench on the halfway line. He then moved to a newspaper in Nottingham where in 1883 he was reporting on a game between Forest and Dunbarton. 'When Dunbarton were pressing their foes, I stood behind the goal of the visitors and enjoyed a chat with James Macaulay, who left the position of centre forward to become Scotland's most famous custodian. The backs, who I think were Lang and Hutchison, were far away up field and we had a "guid crack" about football.' Imagine that happening today.

The first known press box, built to accommodate football reporters, was created by Celtic in 1894. Providing facilities did not of course mean that reporters would always be kind to the players or the clubs. A report in the *Glasgow Observer and Catholic Herald* in 1898 described in glowing terms the excitement before the Scotland v England match held at Celtic Park, but was not so lyrical about the Scottish team after they'd been beaten 3–1. 'A useless, feckless, jumble of Colossal Frosts. Slow, turgid, nervous, blundering, they made an awful mess of their mission and their name.'

Football writers on local papers, then and now, are not normally so outspoken about players – that is if they want to keep in with their local club and get a nice warm seat in the press box.

Attacking players for being greedy started the moment that players got paid, even when they were on a measly maximum of £4 a week. In 1914, a writer on the *Echo Football Guide* was outraged at a new scheme to give players a small percentage of the fee when transferred, describing it as 'the latest sop to the players'. He was well aware, as presumably all fans were, of the fiddles which went on to get round the maximum wage. 'The man who kicks the ball is not satisfied and he loses no opportunity to demand illegal "back handers".'

He described how in the previous season there had been transfer negotiations which had collapsed. 'Only for the public to be mystified at the last moment by the unaccountable refusal of the men in question to be transferred. It was an open secret that the only reason why these players refused to be transferred was because the club requiring them would not pay an illegal bonus on signing. This demand for "backsheesh" took various forms. For instance, one player demanded a preposterous amount for the removal of his furniture ...' Some things don't change.

The *Echo Football Guide* was published by the *Northern Echo* in Darlington and covered all the local clubs in the North-East. It was small size, easy to fit in a pocket, on cheap paper, but cost only one penny. The 1914 edition had 178 pages, giving full details of the local clubs, their results during the last season, past records, bits of news and information.

Once newspapers saw that football sold copies, local as well as national papers started producing football annuals, aimed at 'anoraks', crammed with information. The first known football annual was edited by our friend Charles Alcock in 1868, *The Football Annual*, continuing till 1908, and was quickly copied by the sporting newspapers. *Athletic News* produced a football annual from 1887 which continues to this day, though under a different banner. In 1946 it became *The Sunday Chronicle Football Annual* and is now the *News of the World Football Annual.* (The cover of its 2003–4 edition states that it is in its 117th year of publication, which is technically true, and still a bargain at £5.99 for over five hundred pages.) Even shops got in on the act, ones which specialised in football equipment, such as Gamages. Its annual *Gamages Association Football Annual* was produced from 1909 to 1929 and was considered one of the finest football yearbooks.

Newspapers quickly moved on from covering football in their daily and Sunday editions, plus their annuals, to producing a special Saturday-evening post-match edition, usually known as the 'Pink Un' or 'Green Un'. They were printed so quickly that supporters could buy them on the way home or in the pub that evening and read about the game. Match reports were dictated on the phone, move by move, as it was happening, before the reporter knew what the final score would be, so sometimes they did not make a lot of sense. All the same, they were miracles of production, using laborious old fashioned printing methods with hot metal letters. They mostly died out in the 1970s. Despite the wonders of modern technology, there are no Saturday-evening football papers in Britain today. Alas.

The language of the early football reports reflected the language of the day – players were full of dash, had champion games, were capital players.

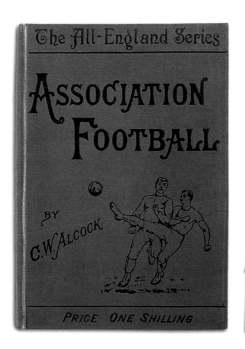

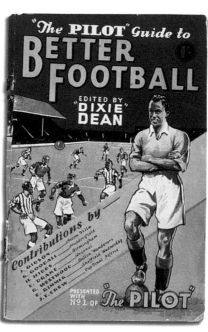

LEFT Football books in the early decades of football were of a very high quality, well produced and well written, such as Charles Alcock's *Association Football* which appeared in 1906. Later books were cheaply produced and written.

OPPOSITE Boys comics with a football theme such as *Champion*, continued through the war, despite the nasty interuptions.

But they also created the first football cliches, such as goalkeepers always being described as 'custodians of the net' and centre forwards as 'net finders'. Some match reports contained expressions which have now disappeared. In that 1914 *Northern Echo*, it was said of Sunderland that their, 'skimble skamble forward work last season was annoying'. But a lot of the expressions and sentiments used in football reporting in the past still remain – there are players still 'grafting hard' and big transfers turning out to be 'flops'.

BALLS AND BIBLIOPHILES

Football in literature, as opposed to the popular prints, which is not to suggest that one is a higher art than the other, goes back many centuries. One of the earliest references to football in England appeared in verse, in a

ABOVE Newspapers and magazines moved on from producing football editions to football annuals, often two hundred pages long, stuffed with fascinating facts, which sold for only a few pennies.

One of the laughs in
"FIREWORKS FLYNN—Prisoner of War"

poem written in 1514 by Alexander Barclay. The poem 'Eche Time and Season', 20 lines long, is about the delights which come round each winter when men 'get the bladder and blow it great and thin'.

Shakespeare has four lines about football in *The Comedy of Errors*, written in 1593, having fun with the symbolism in football.

Am I so round with you as you with me
That like a football you do spurn me thus?
You spurn me hence, and will spurn me hither
If I last this service, you must case me in leather.

Samuel Pepys in 1665 records that he came across a game of football in Covent Garden, where he had gone to dinner in the Piazza. 'The street being full of footballs, it was a great frost.' Again, football was being played as a winter game. Covent Garden seems to have been a popular place for a kickabout, according to John Gay in his 1716 poem, 'Covent Garden'.

The prentice quits his shop, to join the Crew
Increasing Crowds the flying Game persue
Thus as you roll the Ball o'er snowy ground
The gath'ring Globe augments with ev'ry Round.

In fiction, Arnold Bennett has a long description of a game involving Manchester Rovers in his 1912 novel *The Matador of the Five Towns*, while in the *Good Companions*, published in 1930, J. B. Priestley's fictional team is called Bruddersford United.

In poetry and fiction, football was usually mentioned only in passing, so which was the first ever whole book about football? Depends what you mean by football, and what you mean by a book. The experts at the National Museum of Football at Preston think that a 1580 Italian book about calcio, as played in Florence, is probably the first known football book, but they were not playing football as we know it. The early football annuals produced by newspapers were small, softback publications, paperback booklets rather than bound books.

A couple of small books about football appeared in 1867, just four years after the FA was formed, but the person usually credited with writing the first proper football book is our old friend Charles Alcock with his book *Our Winter Game*, 139 pages long, which appeared in 1874. He later wrote or contributed to other football books.

Sir Montague Sherman wrote one of the earliest histories of the game as part of the Badminton library of books about sports which came out first in

LEFT *Roy of the Rovers* first appeared in *Tiger* in 1954, going on to star in his own magazine.

1887. It was unusual in containing real action photographs of players heading or saving the ball, which look amusing today but were technological breakthroughs at the time.

The three best early books about football, prized by all collectors, admired by all football historians, are firstly *The Association Game and the Men who Made It* by Gibson and Pickford, which came out in 1905–6 in

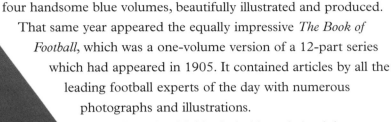

four handsome blue volumes, beautifully illustrated and produced. That same year appeared the equally impressive *The Book of Football*, which was a one-volume version of a 12-part series which had appeared in 1905. It contained articles by all the leading football experts of the day with numerous photographs and illustrations.

The other highly desirable early book is an illustrated one, *Famous Footballers 1895–96* edited by Alcock and Hill, which came out in 1897. It had previously been a weekly series. The one-volume book edition was large format, very expensively produced with 224 stunning photographs of football players and teams, plus a few rugby players.

Despite modern printing methods, no one has ever bettered the quality of production of the early football books of the 1900s. The style and quality and expense of them reflects the style and quality of the authors and also the public they were aimed at – books by gentlemen for gentlemen. They were meant to grace the coffee tables of the time – appearing on the mahogany shelves in a gentleman's study or in the library at his country home.

It was the amateur, public-school players who had founded the game and when they came to look back on these early decades and the early stars and teams they did so nostalgically, fondly remembering the grand old game, rather regretful about so many aspects of the modern, professional, mechanical, mass-market football industry.

After the First World War, these high-class books by high-class persons ceased to appear, and the period from 1918–45 was a relatively barren one for quality football books. The millions on the terraces lapped up the sporting newspapers, the cheaply printed annuals, quickly produced booklets, but didn't seem interested in settling down to a properly produced, solid hardback book. Catton's *Wickets and Goals* in 1926 was an exception, but its contents were mainly about the pre-war era. The working classes, so the old boys moaned, had taken over the game, and it showed. While cricket attracted fine writers, who were writing for people of refined manners and education, football was seen as a plebeian activity. In the newspapers, flowery prose and fine writing might be devoted to the beauty of cricket, but football writing became much simpler and more direct, concentrating on personalities, money and rows.

ABOVE Possibly the best, most desirable set of football books ever – the four-volume *Association Football and the Men who Made It* published in 1905–6.

Football writing aimed at boys had poured out in a steady stream from the 1890s. *Chums and Magnet*, the *Captain* and *Boy's Own Paper* and other boys magazines and comics usually featured at least one football story or serial, often with a football scene on the cover. There were also countless annuals and hardback books featuring football stories. Many of these were classed as budget books, which usually meant a good-quality, full-colour on the cover, but the paper inside was cheaper and the illustrations poorer.

After the First World War, football writing for boys, however, continued to flourish and the public-school settings and ethos remained throughout the 1920s and 1930s, with most football stories being set in boarding schools, about exciting house matches, fags and prefects, despite the fact that most readers had no experience of them. So, while the public-school influence had disappeared from professional football, it lived on for another 50 years in football fiction.

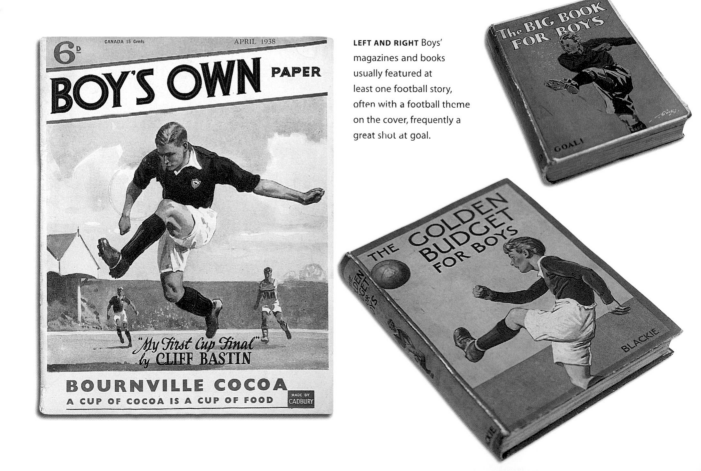

LEFT AND RIGHT Boys' magazines and books usually featured at least one football story, often with a football theme on the cover, frequently a great shot at goal.

OFFICIAL   PROGRAMME

THE FOOTBALL ASSOCIATION INTERNATIONAL MATCH

ENGLAND v SCOTLAND

IN THE EMPIRE STADIUM, WEMBLEY

6D.

*Bovril puts **Beef** into you!*

A TEASPOONFUL TO BOILING WATER & ST...

BOVRIL

Football and Advertising: Medicines Cashing In

7

WHEN FOOTBALL, as we know it, began, and quickly became successful, with people paying to watch it and people being paid to play it, there was immediately created a football industry. At its base were the shop-floor workers, i.e. the players, and the management staff, such as the club secretary (which was how the team manager was described in the early decades), plus trainers and groundsmen and turnstile men. Then there were the manufacturers, wholesalers and retailers, producing football equipment for the professionals and the millions playing it for fun. Newspapers sold more copies, employed specialist reporters, spawned special publications, all on the back of football, all the direct result of football existing, becoming a mass entertainment.

There were also hundreds of indirect spin-offs, benefiting people whose business was not football, but who made it their business to appeal to football players and fans, catering for their interests and attention, getting themselves somehow connected or associated with football, using it for their own aims. Today the greater football industry is colossal, with billions coming in from football merchandising, television rights, sponsorship deals, but right from the beginning, people realised there was money to be made from football.

The success of football helped local transport, as buses and trains put on extra services for match days. Special local and long-distance fares were offered, special excursions organised, just for football fans. In London in the 1920s, there were Saturday fares of one shilling for the whole day on LCC trams, just to get fans to their favourite football grounds. The success of a club, and the thousands of fans coming to see the team play, helped local pubs who made a feature of their nearness to the ground. In Edinburgh in the 1890s, the Vale of Leven Spirit Vaults was advertising that the results of

OPPOSITE For a prestigious game, at a famous stadium, the football authorities did not usually allow commercial firms to blazon their products on the front covers of their official programmes. But Bovril managed it in 1932 for the annual England v Scotland international.

football matches would be 'communicated to their establishments by telephone'. At least one hundred years before lads flocked to pubs to watch wide screens, you could sit in a pub and hear if not actually see the results.

When clubs became limited companies, from around 1900, and issued shares, they made a point of saying how good football was for local business generally. A 1905 brochure for Hearts, the Edinburgh club, that tried to tempt potential investors, said that 'many thousands are brought into the city through the medium of football and, as a consequence, shopkeepers benefit largely'.

Companies specialising in manufacturing turnstiles appeared, printers turned out football programmes and tickets, engineers and builders offered pavilions and then grandstands. Jewellers made and sold cups and medals and trophies not just for the big famous clubs but also for little local village clubs holding their own little competitions.

Restaurants and caterers, inside and outside the ground, began specialising in refreshments for the weary football supporter. Football club dinners, with the directors treating themselves and others rather handsomely if the team had done well, were often very lavish affairs.

TONICS, PILLS AND POTIONS

In theory, the new sport of football was a 'Manly Game', played by hearty public-school chaps or hardy professionals who would, allegedly, carry on with a broken leg rather than let the side down, the sort you would not ever expect whinge or moan about aches and pains. And yet one of the biggest industries which grew up around football was the medicinal. It was not quite on the scale of the equipment-manufacturing industry, but the range and variety and expense of the patent medicines and treatments were just as extensive.

Manufacturers of herbal potions, patent pills and unique mixtures promised instant cures for football knocks, strains and bruises. Elliman's Embrocation was especially popular as was Sloans Liniment and for decades their advertisements appeared in football programmes and football papers.

'This knee is always letting me down. I wish I had used Sloans Liniment before the match,' says a footballer in a 1930s advertisement. That particular footballer was not named, there was just a drawing of an anonymous player, but well-known players and officials were used, and paid

LEFT The success of football helped local transport, as buses and trains put on extra services for match days. Special local and long-distance fares were offered, special excursions organised, just for football fans.

for their endorsements. In 1923, Sanitas Embrocation included a testimonial
from Chas Paynter, West Ham's trainer, who raved about Sanitas. 'It is
wonderfully soothing after an athletes' strenuous exertions!' West Ham
players exerting themselves? Those were the days.

Tonics, alcoholic and otherwise, were highly recommended by experts
with lots of letters after their names. Famous teams, as we know, practically
lived on Oxo from the 1900s. These products were aimed at footballers,
professional and otherwise, also the public at large, the implication being
that if it was good for the health of the footballers, it must be good for you.
'Drink OXO for stamina. OXO plays a manly and important part in the
everyday lives of our leading players,' said an advert in 1911. 'Remember,
the English Cup was won in 1911 for the fifth year in succession by a team
trained on OXO.'

But there were also products aimed purely at the fans. Football grounds,
being very chilly places in bad weather, with fifty thousand perhaps
standing exposed to the elements, caused fans to get aches and pains,
wheezes and coughs as well, so sensible supporters sucked Zubes or other
cough sweets and wrapped up with a good muffler.

LEFT Manufacturers of herbal
potions, patent pills and
unique mixtures promised
instant cures for football
knocks, strains, bruises and
aching muscles. Sloans
Liniment was advertised in
football programmes and
magazines for decades.

George Cohen Fulham F.C. and England player —
says

"Elliman's rub is a must"

Read what George Cohen says about Elliman Athletic Rub "Prior to each game—League, Cup or International, I use Elliman's oils. A few minutes before entering the field a gentle massage with Elliman's Rub is both vital and stimulating for my legs. It is a 'must' in my pre-match preparations."

George Cohen

You, too (even if you're not a star-class footballer!) will find Elliman Athletic Rub vital for warding off aches, sprains, stiffness and for keeping you fit. 3/- from Chemists.

Elliman ATHLETIC RUB

Published for The Football Association by William Heinemann Ltd., 15–16 Queen Street, Mayfair, London, W.I.
Printed in Great Britain by William Clowes and Sons, Limited, London and Beccles

LEFT Elliman's Athletic Rub, like Sloans Liniment, was another popular medicine for football aches, and in the 1960s they even got George Cohen, star of England's World Cup win, to say how wonderful it was.

In the 1911–12 *Morning Leader Football Annual*, there was an advert headed 'Damp Grounds – Cold Winds. Football spectators run greater risks than players. For coughs and colds, take Owbridge's Lung Tonic.' In the same issue, Dr J. Collis Browne was advertising his Chlorodyne, boasting that it was 'the best remedy for coughs, colds, asthma, bronchitis, spasms, hysteria, palpitation, neuraligia, gout, rheumatism and acts like a charm in diarrhoea, cholera and dysentery.' That just covers about everything a fan might ever suffer from.

In the *Athletics News Football Annual* for 1930–1, the latest patent medicine appears to be Rheumogen, billed as the footballer's best friend as 'its heat-generating ointment treats bad knocks in minutes'. Even better, according to an advert a few pages later, was 'Phosferine – The Greatest of All Tonics' for, well, just about everything. It was endorsed by T.G. Bromilow, 'the famous International and Liverpool footballer' who in his photograph, kicking a ball, looks a bit plump, but he swears Phosferine is absolutely essential if you want to keep in 'Tip Top Form'.

As for soothing the nerves, or relaxing after a game, what better way to do so than with a fag. Smoking was presented as a sporting activity – something which sportsmen did, players and spectators alike. Jones of Spurs in his 1904 book might have been personally against his players smoking, but the general impression for the next fifty years or so, according to the advertisements, was that smoking was good for players and spectators alike.

In the 1930s, the Phillips company had a cigarette called BDV Sports, Pure Virgin Blend. If you smoked 75 packs, and kept the packets, you could get a free all-wool muffler in the colours of your favourite club. What a bargain. If after smoking 75 packets you had a bit of a sore throat, what better than an all-wool muffler to make you feel better.

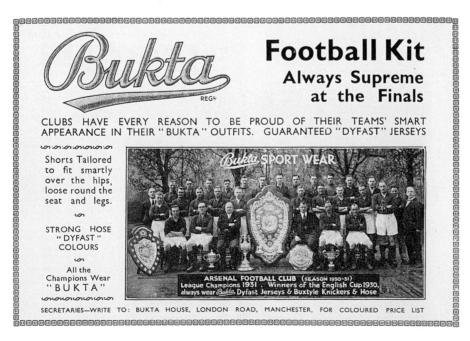

LEFT So that's how Arsenal won the Cup and League in the 1930s – they were wearing Bukta jerseys and shorts, as all champions did.

Tottenham Hotspur Football and Athletic Company, Ltd.

Official Programme

And Record of the Club.

Issued every Match Day. **PRICE ONE PENNY.**

Vol. III. No. 1. SEPTEMBER 1, 1910.

AND SO SAY ALL OF US!

CRICKETER : "Well Cocky, au revoir, and I sincerely hope the weather will be kinder to you than it has been with me."

COCKY : "Carried unanimously."

C. Coventry, Trade Union Printer, Lower Tottenham.

Football Merchandise: Programmes, Toys and Cigarette Cards

8

THE SLOWEST, DOPIEST PEOPLE to realise the fortunes available in football were the football authorities themselves. They cut themselves off from most commercial merchandising and advertising possibilities, feeling above such sordid, mercenary worlds, not wanting their pure game, which they perceived as a labour of love, to be tainted by nasty commerce.

Perhaps, of course, it wasn't doziness. The successful clubs had quite enough money swilling around anyway, so did not need to look for or contemplate any ancillary enterprises. This may be tied in with one of the unexplained questions in football – where did all the money go? When the crowds in the 1920s and 1930s were fifty or sixty thousand, and the players on meagre wages, what happened to all the money? The clubs always maintained it went back into the game, enabling them to keep beating transfer records, expand their grounds, without having to worry about other streams of revenue.

THE MATCH-DAY PROGRAMME

For almost the first hundred years, the only item of what we would now call football merchandising, a product aimed specifically at football fans and produced directly by the clubs themselves, was the match programme. Not that they exactly knocked themselves out to cater for the supporters, either with information or entertainment. At first, most programmes were little more than a team sheet, a one-page card with the names of the players on one side, and perhaps upcoming fixtures on the reverse.

One of the earliest programmes, mentioned already in relation to that 1875 game in Glasgow between Wanderers and Queen's Park, does not have a price, so it was presumably free, perhaps given out to invited guests.

In 1891, for a game at Plumpstead in London, between Heart of Midlothian and Royal Arsenal, the programme was a single sheet, with the teams on one side, plus a poem of welcome to the visitors. On the other side were four small advertisements for local traders. Someone had clearly realised that charging for advertising space could pay for the programme.

One of Manchester United's earliest known programmes, from 1897 when they were still known as Newton Heath, is a one-sheet programme for a game against Walsall, held at Walsall, with three adverts on the back, two for harness and saddle manufacturers and the other for a local printer. The programme itself would appear to have been free.

In the first known programme issued for a Tottenham Hotspur match, against Old St Marks at Northumberland Park in 1893, it made a point of saying it was the 'FIRST' official programme and that it was 'GRATIS' – but in future they would be charging one penny.

By 1900, most programmes were a penny, and most contained adverts. Once they started charging money and selling advertising space, it was realised they should be a bit more than just a team sheet, and should appear value for money, so they now carried bits of club information. Liverpool's first programme, issued in 1892 for a visit by Rotherham Town, was priced at one penny, gave details of the teams and coming fixtures, and also included a small feature called 'Notes'.

For the 1906–7 season, Aston Villa produced a multi-paged programme grandly called *The Villa News and Record*. It was priced at one penny, but sold far more copies than the old team sheets had ever done, which pleased the advertisers. Most of the other leading clubs soon copied the format.

The pre-First World War programmes are fascinating to read for the local advertisements as much as the football, reflecting what was happening in the locality. The programmes for the Glasgow clubs contained adverts for shipbuilders on the Clyde, who wanted workers. In Birmingham there were adverts for cycle, motorbike and motor car manufacturers. In the Sheffield programmes, which were up to 16 pages by 1910, there were always adverts for razor blades. Beer and cigarette advertisements were prominent everywhere, as were local theatres, hoping that football fans would go on to the music hall after the game.

Chelsea were producing a particularly entertaining programme in the mid-1900s. In November 1907 for a Division One game against Blackburn Rovers, the eight-page programme had a cartoon on the front, lots of

football news, statistics, plus jokes, competitions and poems. The poems, written by fans, were parodies of nursery rhymes, all about Chelsea players.

One of the news stories was about an exceedingly quick transfer which had just taken place. 'When Bob Mackie stepped on the field of play for Leicester Fosse against Derby County, less than 24 hours had elapsed since the opening of negotiations by the Fosse secretary – over the "phone".' The mention of the phone was to show how up to date they were.

There was a witty description of five Swaziland chiefs who had been to a recent Chelsea match and who had asked, allegedly, what the players were fighting for on the pitch. 'For more wives perhaps?' The programme included a warning about buying pirate programmes – i.e., any being produced and sold by other people – which suggests that programme sales must have been lucrative enough to have encouraged unofficial versions. One of the advantages of buying a programme, apart from the news and fun, was to check on the codes for the half-time scores. A full list of them appeared in that 1907 Chelsea programme. The scoreboard had been put up courtesy of *The Football Evening News*, so the programme stated, thus saving the club some money.

Another factor increasing overall sales of programmes was the virtual doubling of the number of league clubs in the 1920s when the Third Division (North) and Third Division (South) were formed. Even relatively small clubs, with small gates, managed to produce a reasonable programme. In fact, very often small clubs had bigger, better programmes than so-called bigger, better clubs. Bristol City in the 1930s, for example, had 32-page programmes while Spurs normally had only four pages, with the contents very dull and prosaic, though the cartoon cover, showing a cockerel, was usually amusing.

All the leading football clubs from the 1900s onwards were making a good income from their programmes, thanks to the large crowds and the amount of advertisements. The production of many of them was usually sub-contracted let to local printers, who organised the adverts. And yet when it came to the biggest games of all, the FA Cup Final, which as we know was attracting gates of over 100,000 from 1901, the FA appears not to have made a penny. There was a team sheet for that final between Spurs and Sheffield United, but it appears to have been free, probably just handed to VIPs (one sold for £14,400 at Sotheby's in 2003). Until 1920, it was left to outside commercial enterprise to produce FA Cup Final programmes,

LEFT England v Scotland at Wembley, 1947. This programme was dull and thin, just 12 pages, compared with the more attractive Wembley programmes of the 1920s.

such as WH Smith and *The People* newspaper, selling them to fans in the streets or the railway stations.

The first officially sold programme for an FA Cup Final appeared in 1921 – for the Spurs v Wolves game at Stamford Bridge. This was a very artistic affair with some very high-class artwork on the cover, showing the mythical figure of Victory, holding up the cup, a ball at her feet. It had 18 pages and cost sixpence, a large amount, when normal club programmes were still only one or two pennies.

For the first Wembley Cup Final in 1923, they wanted a suitably imposing programme for such a grand occasion. It ran to 28 pages and was lavish in its contents and the flowery prose extolling the wonders of the Empire and the new Wembley Stadium. 'The Greatest Arena in the World – the largest, the most comfortable, best equipped, holds more than 125,000

and in area it equals the Biblical city, Jericho.' I wonder who measured Jericho for them?

During the depression years of the 1930s, despite strikes and unemployment, football programmes kept up their size, as did attendances at the major football games. Even in hard times, people found money to go to football.

One of the strangest developments in football programmes occurred in the city of Liverpool. At first, the two big clubs, Everton and Liverpool, issued their own, separate programmes, but from 1904 for the next 30 years there was a joint programme. 'The only programme published by the authority of Everton and Liverpool football clubs.' It usually had 16 pages and contained theatre and film news as well as football chat. The advertisements ranged from beer and clothes to extraction of teeth by gas.

Depending on whose first team was at home each Saturday, that team would get the biggest coverage, but in each programme the other club's reserve team would also be featured. A column called 'Everton Jottings' was written by Blue Shirt while 'Anfield Happenings' was written by Red Shirt. It meant that the identical programme was on sale at both football grounds at the same time and to each set of fans. Being at either side of Stanley Park was of course a help when it came to sales and distribution. It was a sensible arrangement, reducing costs, but it is hard to believe that any two rival city clubs would contemplate it today. By the Second World War, however, both Liverpool and Everton had gone back to producing their own individual club programmes.

POSTCARDS, CIGARETTE CARDS AND UNOFFICIAL MERCHANDISE

Football programmes were produced and controlled more or less from the beginning by the clubs themselves. But there was a great deal of unofficial football merchandising which appeared on the market as soon as football became fashionable. Various anonymous Staffordshire pottery firms were turning out cheap mugs with a football theme transferred on to the sides from the 1860s. Better-quality commemorative goods were made from the 1890s when clubs started winning things and wanted to give medals or dishes to their players and officials, though these were not available to the public. But by the 1900s there were lots of football plates and dishes on sale generally. Goss and other firms produced little ornaments with a football theme.

OPPOSITE One of the most unusual programmes was that being produced jointly by Everton and Liverpool in 1910. The same programme served both clubs, giving first-team news of one with the reserve-team news of the other, depending on who was at home. If only rival clubs could be as cooperative today.

Postcard mania started around 1900, when thousands of cheap but well-produced picture postcards came flooding out, many of them showing football teams and players. The impetus was the decision by the Post Office in 1894 to allow commercially produced pictorial cards to go through the post. Until then, the only postcards which existed were those produced by the Post Office. The mania was also helped by improved printing and photographic developments. The quality of these postcards, right up to the 1920s, was excellent.

It wasn't just professional teams who appeared on postcards, but also teams from local leagues, schools, services, villages. Players bought copies for themselves, to send to their mums or girlfriends. There were also humorous cards and birthday cards for boys with a football theme.

Toys with a football theme were in existence from the 1860s. Toy manufacturers who kept up to date with the latest printing methods could easily adapt a football motif to hoops and kites and figures. It was relatively easy to produce a board game based on horseracing, with a dice and some cut-out figures of horses, but more complicated to create a game based on football, with the problem of scoring goals and having two sides of 11 players. The oldest known table football game was made in Preston, home of the Invincibles, in 1884. There were lots of attempts to make mechanical footballers, using strings and levers, but one of the most popular football games was the simplest – Blow Football. The football game which eventually came to dominate the market, at least till the advent of video games, was Subbuteo, devised in 1947 by Peter Adolph in his home in Tunbridge Wells. He was a keen bird watcher and took the name from the Latin for hobby hawk. Since its first appearance, it has been estimated that Subbuteo has so far sold over 500 million sets in over fifty countries.

The most common and most popular item which cashed in on football, using it as a selling tool, was the cigarette card. It's estimated that between 1900 and 1939 over ten thousand different cards were produced with a football theme. As for the total number, they must run into several billion.

Cigarette cards had their origins in France in the mid-nineteenth century when they were little more than trade visiting cards, given out by shops and department stores like Bon Marche, handed to customers for free and purely as a form of advertising.

They gave the shop's name and listed some of their main lines, such as cigarettes. They were pretty and well produced, people liked them, kept them lying around, even collected them. Their use spread to the USA where in the 1880s a tobacco company came up with the idea of putting the cards inside their own packets, not relying on retailers to do so, where they also acted as a 'stiffener', a normally blank piece of cardboard shoved into a pack of cigarettes to keep it from being crushed. Other tobacco companies in the USA soon followed, notably Duke, printing on them pretty illustrations.

BELOW The football game which eventually came to dominate the market, at least till the advent of video games, was Subbuteo, devised in 1947 by Peter Adolph in his home in Tunbridge Wells.

By the 1890s, they had arrived in Britain, with leading cigarette firms like Wills and Ogden's starting to use them. The earliest cigarette cards in the UK featured actresses, soldiers, ships and sportsmen – topics deliberately chosen because most smokers at the time were men. It was in fact small boys who did most of the collecting, swapping the cards or sticking them in albums which the cigarette companies were soon providing. (What a mistake that was, ruining precious items of social history, making it impossible to read the reverse side with its fascinating football facts. Stuck-in cards are now far less valued. Today, collectors want un-stuck-in cards which they carefully put in see-through plastic albums, oh, so much better).

Amongst the earliest cards to feature footballers were sets from Ogden's in 1896, Kinnear in 1898 and Marcus's 1898. There were at the time hundreds of different little cigarette manufacturers all over the country and all with their own brands.

Then came the Tobacco War of the 1900s. It originated in the USA where five of the leading companies combined to form the American Tobacco Company and started buying up other firms. They expanded into the UK in 1901, where they bought Ogden's. Other UK firms responded, 13 of the leading ones forming themselves into the Imperial Tobacco Company. That was when the war began in earnest, with the two groups bidding to outdo the other. One of their sales tools was more and better cigarette cards, particularly those featuring football, which was now being followed by millions. The quality of the cards was exceptional, right through the 1920s, notably

those produced by Wills, Players, Gallaher, Churchman, Phillips. Between 1922 and 1923, Godfrey Phillips issued with their Pinnace trade name an astounding total of 2,462 different football cards – in three sizes: miniature, ordinary and cabinet size. Almost every professional footballer alive and every team was covered.

There were also trade cards issued by a variety of firms, from sweets and tea manufacturers to boys' magazines and comics like the *Magnet*, *Gem* and DC Thomson comics, which featured footballers. The idea was the same – giveaways to be collected which would promote sales, but the printing was never quite as good as the classic ciggie cards.

Cigarette cards all but died out with the Second World War, but trade cards have continued, in various forms, coming and going as marketing departments hit on what they think is a brilliant new sales gimmick, producing stickers or collectables portraying famous footballers, without realising it was all done, more or less, and often much better, 100 years ago.

BELOW AND OPPOSITE The most common and most popular item which cashed in on football, using it as a selling tool, was the cigarette card. It's estimated that between 1900 and 1939 over ten thousand different cards were produced with a football theme.

CHURCHMAN'S CIGARETTES

J. E. ATKINSON (BOLTON WANDERERS)

CHURCHMAN'S CIGARETTES

M. BURNS (IPSWICH TOWN)

CHURCHMAN'S CIGARETTES

S. BARTRAM (CHARLTON ATHLETIC)

CHURCHMAN'S CIGARETTES

G. W. HALL (TOTTENHAM HOTSPUR)

Players: Stars and a Famous Manager

9

The heroes of the 1920s included many Scotsmen. They had always been around, a vital part of every leading English club since the beginning of professionalism, most of them small and cunning, either wingers or centre forwards. Some stayed in Scotland and became heroes at home, like Jimmy McGrory of Celtic and Alan Morton of Rangers, but many migrated over the border and became stars in England, including Hughie Gallacher, barely 5ft 6ins high, who played in Scotland for Airdrie before moving to Newcastle.

But the biggest star of the 1920s was Dixie Dean of Everton, one of the earliest English players to become a household name, establishing goal scoring records – 60 goals alone in the 1927–8 season – which have never been beaten. He was christened William Ralph Dean and known to his family and close friends as Bill, but he was always known to the footballing public as Dixie. He had curly black hair and darkish complexion and when playing for his first club, Tranmere, the crowd had given him the nickname Dixie, a convoluted reference to the southern states of the USA, from which of course he had not come. He himself never liked the nickname, but had to live with it. During one game, in which he had humiliated the opposition, a rival supporter had grabbed him and muttered 'We'll get you, you black bastard.' A policeman approached, having heard the threat, but Dean told the officer he need not interfere, he would look after the matter. He then delivered a sudden punch to the man's face, sending him reeling back into the crowd. 'That was a beauty,' said the policeman, 'but I never saw it.'

In the 1930s, a Scotsman, Alex James, with his baggy shorts and shuffling run, was considered the cleverest inside forward ever seen, one of Scotland's Wembley Wizards who thumped England 5–1 in 1928. He began

OPPOSITE Dixie Dean of Everton, goal-scoring machine of the 1920s, came from Birkenhead, and was nicknamed Dixie because of his dark looks. Height, 5 feet, 10 inches; weight, 12 stone, 12 pounds; hobby, training greyhounds.

with Raith Rovers, moved to Preston North End and then on to Arsenal in
1929 for a fee of £9,000, playing in Arsenal's hat-trick of League
championships sides.

I have a pair of Alex James's 1930s boots, one of my many treasured
possessions, in mint condition. Not *his* pair of course, just a line of boots he
gave his name to. The Alex James Boot. I can't see any maker's name – just
Club, Made in England – but his name is stamped inside and on the sole,
with the letters AJ 22.

We tend to think that star players giving their names to a make of boots
is of modern origin, beginning perhaps with Gazza and Beckham, but players have been lending their names to football products from as early as the
1900s, if just as written testimonials, for which presumably they were paid.

But the huge growth of football in the 1920s and 1930s, in gates and
income generated, meant that star players and star teams were signed up

to promote a whole host of products. They didn't have agents as such, but firms would come to them and offer fees or other inducements for their names.

There were Dixie Dean boots being advertised in the 1920s, made by T. Richardson of Northampton. 'Exactly as worn by Dixie Dean during his Record Goal-Scoring Season, 1927–28. Every League player should insist on wearing "The Dixie Dean".'

EARLY ENDORSEMENTS

From the 1930s onwards, FA Cup Final teams usually managed to cash in on their achievements, the whole team being photographed endorsing some product or lending their names, which suggest there must have been an early pool system, the captain perhaps organising the fee then dividing it up. In 1936, the Sheffield United FA Cup Final team were photographed in their best suits sitting round a very phoney-looking breakfast table with a packet of Shredded Wheat in front of each of them. 'Shredded Wheat again in the Cup Final News!' screamed the headline. In 1938, the Huddersfield Town team who got to the FA Cup Final turned out all to be 'enthusiastic users of Watermen's Pens', though in the group photograph only one of them appears to have a pen, using it to sign a football.

In that photograph, one of them can be seen standing holding a cigarette. Footballers of the times were still keen on the odd fag, especially after the game while soaking in a communal bath. Dixie Dean even appeared in cigarette advertising – endorsing Carrcras Club cigarettes, 'the cigarette with a kick in them'. They were a budget brand, aimed at the working man on the terraces, sold at tuppence for five.

Star players were entitled to increase their earnings by any advertising or endorsements they could pick up. In 1920, the players' maximum wage went up from £4 a week to £9 a week–but two years later, it came down to £8 a week during the playing season and £6 a week in the summer. It remained at this level till after the Second World War. It was still roughly around double that of an ordinary skilled worker, and most of the population still considered footballers well off, with a good life, being paid to play football, with the best-known ones enjoying quite a few nice perks.

Writing for newspapers, and even publishing books, provided some extra money for well-known players, even if they didn't do any actual writing, though some did. C. B. Fry, the famous cricketer and footballer of the

1890s, went on to have a sports magazine in his name, which he edited and wrote for, as later on did Charles Buchan, Sunderland, Arsenal and England star of the 1920s, who became a celebrated journalist after he retired and edited *Charles Buchan's Football Monthly,* which ran for many years.

By the 1930s, there had grown up a huge market for football trivia and gossip with many weekly papers and magazines devoting pages to the so-called 'Inside Stories' or 'Intimate Portraits' of our heroes, their hobbies and interests, behind the scenes in their daily lives. Like most people of the time, they seemed to spend two or three nights at the cinema, listening to the radio and also reading books, or so they said. A lot of them had other jobs they did part time, such as running a newsagent's shop, which their wives looked after for the most part but where they would spend an hour or two a day behind the counter, chatting to customers.

Their social status was no better, no higher than it had been before the First World War, but a lot of them, now they had a bit more money from advertising or columns, could afford to dress very well, some of them almost like toffs.

In *The Topical Times* for May 18, 1935, there is a section entitled 'The Swell Guys in Soccer'. The list included Eddie Hapgood, captain of Arsenal and England. 'Always used to pride himself on being the best-dressed footballer in the game. His plus fours are always immaculately cut and his shirts and ties are chosen with great care.' Another was George Barber, who had just been transferred from Luton to Chelsea.

'The week he got his first pay, he went out and bought a neat suiting. With bowler hat and a watch-chain across his middle, he turned up for training. When he opened the door of the dressing room, the boys got a shock. Jack Whitley, popular Chelsea trainer, rubbed his eyes, then he found his voice. "Wrong door m'lord," he said. "Corinthians at the other end!"'

HERBERT CHAPMAN–THE FIRST MODERN MANAGER

Many players naturally hoped to stay on in the profession and become managers, especially after the role of football manager was transformed by Herbert Chapman, the first and in many ways still the greatest of modern managers. Until he came along, the manager-secretary didn't have much power, with the directors often picking the team, controlling money and transfers, even dictating tactics.

Chapman, a Yorkshireman, was born in 1878. In his early years he played as an amateur, a roly-poly inside forward, taking a job as an engineer in whichever town he found himself. For two years he played for Spurs, but not with much distinction, being best known for his lemon-coloured boots. He went into management in 1907 with Northampton but his successful years began when he took over Huddersfield in 1920, winning the FA Cup in 1922 and the league title two years later. He moved to Arsenal in 1925 a club

LEFT Herbert Chapman (right) the first modern manager, with Alex James, centre, and Tom Whittaker, right. Chapman played for Spurs – but made Arsenal into a 1930s legend.

which had so far won nothing, the same year the offside rule was changed so that only two rather than three players were needed to keep a player onside, giving the attacking team an advantage.

Chapman was years ahead in most aspects of the game, insisting that all the Arsenal teams, including youth and reserves, played to the same system. He introduced team numbers on the Arsenal shirts in 1928, many years before it became standard practice, organised team talks every week and changed Arsenal's strip from all red, which they had originally copied from Nottingham Forest, adding white sleeves to make it more distinctive. He was brilliant at spotting and melding talent together and laying down tactics. He perfected a defensive system, having come to the conclusion that 'a team can attack for too long', relying on sudden counter-attacks to do the damage, which led to the myth of 'lucky Arsenal'. He was keen on public relations and was instrumental in getting the name of the local Tube station changed from Gillespie Road to Arsenal. He advocated a single manager for the England national team, instead of a selection committee, which didn't happen for many years, and suggested two referees on the pitch, an idea never taken up yet, but which might be one day.

The Arsenal team under Chapman won the league twice and the cup once and went on to dominate the rest of the 1930s. He died suddenly of pneumonia in 1934 aged 55. A bust of him by Jacob Epstein was placed in Highbury's famous marble hall. No doubt he will still be watching over Arsenal, the club he first raised to greatness, when it moves to its new stadium.

OPPOSITE Arsenal playing Sunderland in 1934. Chapman changed Arsenal's strip from all red, which they had originally copied from Nottingham Forest, adding white sleeves to make it more distinctive.

The Football Pools

THE MOST MONEY OF ALL FROM FOOTBALL made by those not directly involved in the game was made by the football pools. Betting in sport had been there from the beginning, whether prizefighting or horseracing, and the early sporting newspapers were mainly devoted to helping people put bets on horses. Betting on the result of a particular local football match was known to take place in pubs even before football was formalised, before the FA and the Football League got to grips with running the game. When they came along, they were terrified of any sort of betting in football, fearful that bets would lead to players being bribed, results being fiddled, and thus a nonsense being made of their cup and league systems. Once the leagues and cups were established, it was a bit complicated to devise betting systems with so many matches going on, unlike a horse race, with a simple first, second and third being immediately decided.

The idea of the football pools, predicting the results of a set of games as opposed to a one-off, originated in the sporting newspapers and magazines as circulation boosters, to sell more copies and attract attention rather than make money in themselves. In the *Athletics Journal* of 1887, a prize of £2.10 was offered to all readers guessing the correct score on three matches, Sheffield v Notts Rangers, Halliwell v Burnley, Accrington v Bootle. In 1909, the newly launched *Racing and Football Outlook* upped the prizes by offering five guineas every week to anyone who could correctly forecast six teams who would win away from home. It was a huge success, with others quickly following. In 1911, *Umpire* magazine was offering £300 to anyone who could correctly predict the scores of six matches.

Naturally enough, with such massive sums on offer through newspapers and magazines, bookmakers were soon paying big money on similar bets,

OPPOSITE A football pools winner in the 1930s. Littlewood's, and all the other companies, were the biggest winners, making millions, employing thousands, yet for so many years, paying not one penny back to football.

and there arose rumours of match fixing, the first serious claim being made in 1914 about a game between Manchester United and Liverpool. The bookmakers refused to pay up, saying it was a fiddle by a betting syndicate, hatched in a Manchester pub, with bets places all over the country. A football investigation found eight players guilty, four from each side, and they were banned for life. (They were pardoned at the end of the war, having all served their country, which was too late for one of them, killed in action.)

FOOTBALL BETTING BANNED

In 1920, the government banned cash betting on football under the Ready Money Betting Act, though credit betting was still allowed. That seemed to be the end of the bookmakers' involvement in football. Prizes for predicting results were still being offered by newspapers and a practice had grown up by which agents would buy up lots of copies of newspapers, cut out the coupons, and sell them to people.

The first known football pools coupons to be issued separately, and not as part of a newspaper offer, were produced by Frederick Jarvis, a Birmingham bookmaking firm in 1923. They saw the demand for separate coupons and also managed to get round the law as it applied to bookmakers by collecting the money wagered the week *after* the game – i.e., the betting had been on credit. It was such an immediate success, that scores of other firms started printing similar coupons. In under five years it was calculated that more people were filling in football pools than were going to football matches. By the 1930s, there were those who asserted that one of the reasons for the enormous success and popularity of football was the football pools.

The football authorities were aghast. They worried not just about bribery but also about crowd riots. If a game was going unexpectedly the wrong way, ruining everyone's pools coupons, there could well be pitch invasions. They leaned on the government to ban the pools. Legislation was proposed against the pools in 1935, but the pools companies, using their mailing lists, encouraged clients to write to their MPs to complain.

In 1935, Littlewood's were spending a fortune on self-promotion, flying aeroplanes over London with streamers behind the planes announcing 'LITTLEWOOD'S ABOVE ALL', paying for wireless concerts on Radio Luxembourg during which their latest dividends were announced, as well as

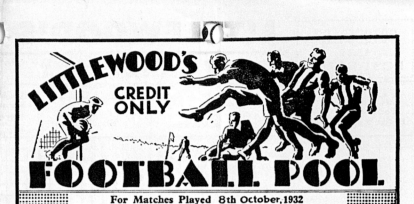

LITTLEWOOD'S CREDIT ONLY FOOTBALL POOL

For Matches Played 8th October, 1932

LITTLEWOOD'S BIG MONEY POOLS

Do you know that last week we paid out over TWO THOUSAND cheques ranging from £7 to £250.

Surely no further Proof is needed that Littlewood's Pools are paying the Biggest Dividends in the Country? Study the figures in the table below— and be convinced. These are the actual Dividends declared for every Pool since the opening of this Season— and remember Every Dividend is declared and certified by an independent firm of Accountants.

Date	Pool 1	Pool 2	Pool 3	Pool 4	Pool 5	Pool 6
Aug. 27	322/-	192/-	350/-	94/-	276/-	75/-
Sept. 3	20/-	83/-	128/-	33/-	115/-	103/-
,, 10	15/-	1025/-	21/-	128/-	106/-	56/-
,, 17	107/-	7100/-	33/-	8090/-	607/-	80/-
,, 24	173/-	50/-	76/-	304/-	1696/-	470/-

Have you entered for our £1,000 Free Competition? If not, start right now. There is absolutely nothing to pay. We offer £1,000 for 18 Correct Results, and if this is not won, then £500 is offered for the next best. Only Littlewood's could organise a Competition like this, and there is no more genuine Competition in the Football World.

£1000 FREE

H. LITTLEWOOD Ltd. - Hood Street, Whitechapel, Liverpool (Comp.)
J. Moores, Director
Copyright: anyone imitating this list will be prosecuted

LEFT In 1935, Littlewood's were spending a fortune on self-promotion, flying aeroplanes over London with streamers behind the planes announcing 'LITTLEWOOD'S ABOVE ALL'.

taking expensive advertisements in all the newspapers, featuring their big winners. In February 1935, a couple from Reading won £5,886 for only 1d and were photographed in the press.

The Football League then thought up a devilish plan to ruin the pools – they would keep the fixtures a secret till the last minute. What cunning. That backfired when the clubs immediately suffered poor gates, with people not knowing in advance who the opposition were going to be. They dropped the idea after only a few weeks of the 1935–36 season.

The pools went from strength to strength. By 1939, £800,000 a week was being collected by the leading companies, notably Littlewood's and Vernons in Liverpool. The government's post offices did huge business as most people sent off their stakes with sixpence and one-shilling postal orders. The football pools industry was employing thirty thousand people,

BELOW Viv Nicholson in 1961 won the then enormous sum of £152,000 on Littlewood's, and went on to spend, spend, spend, till most of it was gone. She later came to visit the street where she lived before striking it rich.

most of them women, far more than all the professional football clubs put together. Football was clearly helping the nation's economy as a whole – though football itself was not gaining one penny. The pools promoters became so cash rich and successful that some, like Littlewood's, were able to branch out into other areas, like shops and mail order.

After the war, when football began again, and supporters flocked back in their millions, the pools companies did even better. In 1948, football was receiving £4 million a year in gate money–while the football pools were taking in over £50 million a year from the eight million punters who filled in their pools each week. The Government was by now making a fortune as well–having imposed a pools tax which netted them £12 million a year. Huge wins were reported in the papers, like Lottery winners in the 1990s, and given massive headlines. In 1950, the biggest win was £100,000. By 1956, it had reached £200,000.

FOOTBALL AUTHORITIES ACCEPT THE INEVITABLE

The pools promoters had for some time been offering the football authorities money, but it had always been refused. Having always come out against gambling on football, they couldn't very well be seen to be profiting from it.

But in 1959, they saw sense. They won a court case which established their copyright on the pools fixture lists. Fixtures could not be printed without their permission. The pools companies then signed a ten-year deal with the Football League whereby they would pay a percentage of their gross takings from football, with a guaranteed minimum of £245,000 a year.

So, finally, in 1959, the football authorities started making money from those making money out of football, something they could well have done up to 60 years earlier. Once the principle was established, their share of the the pools money gradually went up. In 1973, the pools promoters did another deal, agreeing to pay the Football League £23 million over the next 13 years.

What they had done at last was to tap the commercial possibilities of football, a process which was to revolutionise football totally by the end of the century.

1939–2003

PART TWO

The history of football spectators; equipment; merchandising and the media; some post-war famous players, including the arrival of black players and foreign players, not forgetting women players; football and art, then football today; with only a few diversions backwards and forwards.

Post-War Spectators:
From Hooligans to Celebs

11

WHEN THE SECOND WORLD WAR ended in 1945, the crowds flocked back to football in even greater numbers than they had done after the First World War. Other activities and entertainments also attracted huge audiences, whether cinema, dancing, speedway or dog tracks, part of a general enthusiasm to get out and about once more.

With football, records were established which will probably never be beaten. In the first post-war season, 1946–7, English league football attracted 35 million fans, many of them ex-servicemen, compared with 28 million fans before the war. In 1948–9, it reached 41,271,424–a record that still stands to this day.

It hovered around the 40-million mark for a few more seasons, then began a slow decline. By 1956, it had fallen to 33 million. By 1964 it was 27 million. The lowest point came in the 1985–6 season when only 16,488,577 spectators turned up, well under half of the post-war peak.

HOOLIGANISM TAKES HOLD

Where had all the fans gone to in the 1970s and 1980s? Increased leisure and more attractive ways of spending it, such as motor cars, television and foreign holidays, that was one explanation. But the faults and the problems were mostly in football itself, such as hooliganism, which drove decent people away from games.

Organised gangs who deliberately looked for trouble at football matches had appeared in the 1970s. They were actively hoping for a fight with rival supporters, though they did not publicly admit it, usually maintaining that rival gangs had invaded their territory on the terraces, insulted them in some way, were out to harm them, so they needed to get their retaliation in

OPPOSITE British clubs have attempted over the years to introduce a note of glamour and sex appeal into following football and cheer up spectators, but without a great deal of success. Everton did try hard in 1968 before the FA Cup Final against West Brom by parading some lovelies modelling the latest fashions in the club colours. West Brom won 1–0.

first. There was a right-wing, fascist, racist element to many of these gangs, who had infiltrated the terraces for their own purposes, but mostly the gangs were composed of genuine football supporters, who closely followed their teams and their favourite players, travelled long distances to support them, but also happened to like the posing and preening and camaraderie that went with being in a gang-wearing the same scarves, adopting the same skinhead haircut, enjoying the excitement of getting in a skirmish and charging after their hated rivals. Mostly it was little more than playground fighting, with a lot of abuse and chanting, the leaders being urged on by onlookers, but often it did lead to real fights, real injuries, innocent people getting hurt and property damaged.

Adolescent males of the species have always enjoyed being in gangs. A decade or so earlier they might have gone down to Brighton on their scooters. From around the 1890s, as we know, there had always been the drunk and disorderly who followed football, who went on day trips to London and appalled the locals, but until the 1970s they had behaved relatively peacefully at football matches. In some ways, hooliganism was a throwback to folk football, when football had been used as an excuse for violence. With the arrival of violent gangs in football, the police, in theory at least, knew where and when it would happen–in and around certain football grounds–so they could be prepared. But of course it gave football a bad name.

When surveys in the 1970s and 1980s asked people why they had given up going to football, hooliganism was a common and easy answer. Alarmist stories and nasty experiences probably did put off many families. I was taking my own children to games at the time, but I found it easy enough to keep them out of the way when I saw or heard trouble coming down Tottenham High Road. But the experience of going to football was not particularly pleasant anyway. The stadiums were decaying, the food horrible, the conditions squalid, the lavatories smelly with people relieving themselves on the crowded terraces, unable to get out.

Some things were changing. The sight and sound of the police band at Highbury, marching proudly up and down in their finery at half-time, batons being twirled, was left over from another era, now being either ignored or mocked by the young, modern hooligans, till it finally disappeared. The half-time scoreboards eventually went as public address systems improved or fans carried their own transistors. Old ways were fading, but nothing much new or exciting was happening. Going to a football stadium did not seem as appetising or as attractive as once it had.

But I think the major if mostly unstated reason for the decline in popularity was the standard of football itself. After the euphoria of England's World Cup win in 1966, it was soon pretty clear that England and Scotland had been left behind, were second-class citizens of the football world. The home internationals, between the home nations, had lost all appeal and were finally abandoned in 1984–the centenary year of the England v Scotland games which had once captivated both nations. The biennial invasion of the Tartan Army had gone for ever.

It was one thing to watch and be excited by one or two of our teams which were doing well, such as Liverpool, playing excellent football, winning lots of trophies, but lower down the leagues it was clear the standards were poor. Gates in the second, third and fourth divisions were hardest hit. The leading first division clubs in London, Lancashire, Yorkshire, the Midlands and in Glasgow drew support from a wider catchment area, with fans able to travel on the new motorways to matches, but it meant the purely local clubs lost even more of their local support.

PLASTIC PITCHES AND ASTRO-BURNS

Some new, rather desperate methods were adopted in an attempt to modernise football, notably the introduction of artificial pitches. They had been developed in the USA and used there quite successfully, and were meant to eliminate the vagaries of the mud and rain and make the game quicker, more skilful. The first all-weather football pitch, the Astroturf, opened in Islington, London, in 1972. Several professional clubs tried it out and decided to tear up their grass and lay an artificial version. The FA and the Football League, as ever, were nervous about such a change, but gave in with reservations. Queens Park Rangers in 1982 were the first club to transform their pitch, followed by Luton, Oldham and Preston North End. It did seem for a while as if it might be the way forward, and Terry Venables, ever at the cutting edge, co-authored a football novel called *They Used to Play on Grass*.

I played on the Islington Astroturf several times myself, but didn't like it. The ball bounced very high, making it difficult to control, and you ended up with what appeared to be a burn if you tried a sliding tackle. Watching

professionals at Loftus Road, it was clear they didn't much like it either. By the late 1980s, at Loftus Road and elsewhere, plastic grass had gone and real grass had returned.

In the end, we didn't need artificial turf in order to improve playing conditions. One of the many advantages of all the money which came into the game in the 1990s was the wider use of undersoil heating, which had formerly been far too expensive, except for the richest clubs. You rarely ever see goalmouths turning brown and bare, which used to happen in all divisions. Big games no longer get cancelled at the last moment because of a frozen pitch.

HEYSEL AND HILLSBOROUGH PROMPT RETHINK

It was a terrible disaster which would contribute most to the massive improvement in conditions for spectators at our football grounds. While the football authorities were still dithering about how to stop the decline in football attendances or combat hooliganism, issuing reports in the early 1980s with titles like 'Soccer – The Fight for Survival' or so-called blueprints for the future, which mainly seemed concerned with reorganising the leagues, the major clubs were concerned only about their own survival. Then came the Hillsborough disaster of 1989 which shocked the nation. During a semi-final game between Liverpool and Nottingham Forest, 96 people were killed and 150 seriously injured, the worst ever football tragedy in Europe. It came after the 1984 Heysel Stadium disaster in Belgium, which also involved Liverpool fans, and a serious fire at Bradford City's Valley Parade ground.

It was clear from the Taylor Report into Hillsborough that among the contributing factors had been overcrowding on the open terraces and the dilapidated and dangerous state of our ancient football stadiums. A massive government-backed campaign aimed to build new or improved stadiums.

All-seater stadiums were created by the major clubs in the 1990s. Executive boxes were incorporated and hospitality suites for corporate entertaining. I remember at Spurs when the first executive boxes, with room for eight people, went on offer at £13,000 for a season. I thought no one would buy them at that price. But they were snapped up.

All-seater stadiums meant that almost all supporters of our leading clubs had to buy season tickets in advance. You could no longer expect to turn up

on the day and get in. The big clubs might no longer have the vast crowds they had in the 1930s, as capacities had been reduced, but those crowds sat in a great deal more comfort and paid a great deal more money for their seats. By 2003, the leading clubs like Manchester United and Arsenal had ten-year waiting lists of fans waiting to give them money.

After the record low in 1986, total attendances began to climb again, reaching 20 million in 1992, with more women and families coming back into football. They had been there in the early years, as old photographs show, but had begun to disappear by the 1970s. Even more surprising was the increase among middle-class fans who had been all but absent for decades, since the glorious days of the Corinthians and the other amateur sides. The quality were now much more interested in football, which was how it had all begun.

ABOVE Then came the Hillsborough disaster of 1989 which shocked the nation. During a semi-final game between Liverpool and Nottingham Forest, 96 people were killed and 150 seriously injured, the worst ever football tragedy in Europe.

FROM SOVEREIGNS TO STREAKERS

Celebrity spectators started with the Royal Family in 1892 when the Prince of Wales agreed to become the first royal patron of the FA, but he didn't actually turn up to a game, not even when he became Edward VII. The first visit by a king was in 1909 when George V went to an England v Scotland game–and in 1914 he attended the FA Cup Final. His presence at the first Wembley Cup Final in 1923 was said to have been a factor in preventing a major tragedy when the crowd spilled on to the pitch.

Since then there has been a royal, if not always the monarch, at every Cup Final. All the same, our first family appears not to have been at all interested in football, turning up as a duty and much preferring horseracing, until quite recently. Prince William and Prince Harry are known to be football fans, with Prince Harry often being spotted in the crowd at Highbury to watch Arsenal, which has long had royal connections. In a smart bit of public relations, Arsenal got the then Prince of Wales to open in its new West Stand in 1932.

RIGHT Footballers' wives always add a bit of glamour and style to any occasion. Before their FA Cup Final of 1971 against Arsenal, the wives and girlfriends of the Liverpool team lined up in two rows in the traditional formation, showing some decidedly Sixties short skirts, boots and haircuts. Arsenal won 2–1.

Politicians have often popped up at football games, if only to keep in with their public. Winston Churchill, who had no interest in football, was presented to the teams before England played Scotland in 1941, part of his war effort to boost morale. Field Marshall Montgomery, when not fighting the war, was a fan of Portsmouth and was often seen at their games. Harold Wilson tried to make political capital by claiming that England only ever won the World Cup under a Labour Government, true but not quite connected though he was a genuine fan of Huddersfield Town. When I interviewed him once, I was unable to stop him reciting all the players from their pre-war teams. He wrote me a letter afterwards in which he mentioned the 1938 FA Cup Final when Preston beat Huddersfield with a last-minute penalty–then in handwriting, he added 'after hitting the crossbar'. Tony Blair always maintained he was a fan of Newcastle United, his boyhood team, but was rarely seen at games, though he did feature in a photo opportunity at Downing Street, heading a ball with Kevin Keegan. Abroad, foreign politicians have often tried to turn football to their advantage. Mussolini was

LEFT Celebrity supporters – or at least well-known people who just happened to show an interest in football. The Queen demonstrates her table football skills in 1955.

RIGHT None of the Beatles was ever interested in football, but Paul McCartney turned up at Wembley in 1968 to see Everton get beaten 1–0 by West Brom.

determined that Italy should win the 1934 World Cup, seeing it as a propaganda coup for his regime, and was said to threaten dire consequences if they didn't win it – which they did. The England team while playing in Germany in 1937 were forced to give the Nazi salute, the British ambassador saying it would give offence to Hitler otherwise, but they did manage to beat the Germans 6–3.

Over the decades, endless showbusiness celebrities, ranging from Gracie Fields to Marilyn Monroe have turned up at football matches, often being invited to kick off a match. There have been many male stars connected with individual clubs, such as George Robey, who had once been a Millwall player, Tommy Trinder at Fulham, and Elton John at Watford.

Glamour girls in the form of US-style cheerleaders were introduced at Bristol City in the 1970s, but have never caught on in Britain. Club mascots, wearing silly outfits, were occasionally seen pre-war, and are now common at many clubs.

LEFT As not seen on TV. Streakers first appeared on the pitch at football matches in 1981, but TV cameras soon learned to avert their gaze.

A new addition to the ranks of ordinary spectators occurred in 1981, something never seen at a football ground before, or at least not recorded–streakers. Rugby got in first, with Erika Roe running naked across the pitch at Twickenham, but a week later Variania Scotney, a 17-year-old waitress, ran topless across the pitch at Highbury during an Arsenal v Spurs game. Her performance earned her a place on page three of the *Daily Mirror*. Since then, there have been many sightings of streakers, male and female, at football matches, but you have to be there to see them. Television has got wise to it, and cuts to other cameras.

Equipment

12

WHAT A LOT OF TROUBLE the ball used to cause. Not just its weight when it got wet, or heading it if you hit the lace, but losing it. As late as 1946, during an FA Cup Final between Derby and Charlton, it was still bursting in vital games. Five days later, in a league game between the same two teams, the ball burst again. There were also delays when some defender hoofed it miles over the stand and out of the ground or into the river, as happened at Nottingham Forest and elsewhere. There never seemed to be enough balls in those days, even at top clubs, so everyone had to wait till it was returned or a new one found. Today, at even apparently impecunious clubs, it often seems to be raining balls. A new one will appear even for throw-ins if it looks as if there might be the slightest delay. Games sometimes get stopped because there are two balls on the pitch, rather than none at all. And they don't burst any more, though they can go a bit soft.

BALLS, BLADDERS AND BLARNEY

The inflatable bladder began to disappear from the 1950s and a valve meant there was no the need to lace up a ball any more. Synthetic, non-porous materials improved water resistance, so balls ceased to get heavier in wet weather. A white ball was used for floodlit games in the 1950s, and an orange one when there was snow or frost, but until 1963, a football was still its traditional colour of deep brown. That all changed after the World Cup of 1970 when the white leather ball developed by Adidas, with its black pentagons, became the norm for all professional and amateur games.

There have been other developments since then, by various manufacturers, all claiming to have produced the latest in high technology, making balls faster, easier to bend, more aerodynamic. Many of their

OPPOSITE The Tornado boots designed in Austria in 1958 by a former referee called Englebert Harmer. Lightweight boots appeared on the Continent long before they were accepted in England, and for years were dismissed as slippers, more suitable for girls or ballet dancers than real men.

scientific claims and much of the technical language is reminiscent of what ball manufacturers were saying a hundred years ago, amazing us or confusing us with their latest astounding developments.

For the 2002–3 season, the ball used in the Premier League was something called the Nike Geo Merlin Vapor ball. According to one description, it 'incorporated refined DART – Dynamic Acceleration Response and Touch – technology and had a modified carbon latex 6 wing bladder to provide greater rebound properties and an AirBloc valve system to provide superior air retention'. The ball retailed at £50. It's not cheap, if you want the very latest in ball technology.

It's often said that all modern balls are lighter, and modern players do seem to be able to thump it enormous distances, especially goalkeepers, but that is more a matter of the strength and technique of the modern player, plus the consistency and aerodynamics of the modern ball. In fact they are not appreciably lighter than they were hundred years ago. They just keep their weight and shape better.

BOOTS ... FROM CLOGS TO SLIPPERS

The change in the football boot has been more dramatic. They were like heavy-duty clogs in the olden days, with their specially strengthened toe caps and high sides. Now they are more like slippers.

Lighter boots were first used abroad during the 1930s, and though some appeared here, they didn't catch on in Britain, being rather scorned, dismissed as merely fit for girls or playing in the sun on the beach, not for real men on real pitches. Our pitches did of course become like quagmires in winter, even at the best-cared-for grounds.

In the Hampden Park programme for the international between Scotland and England in 1937 there is a page marked 'Soccer Items in Brief' which contains an item about boots. 'When the Hungarians opposed England at Highbury on December 2, 1936, they wore football boots weighing 1 pound each. The weight of a football boot worn by a British player is 3 pounds.'

The difference in weight is remarkable. No comment was added to this amazing fact, but the unspoken reaction was presumably on the lines of what funny foreigners, don't they wear silly boots, you won't catch us wearing them over here.

Even after the Second World War, when we were playing European sides again, famous players like Billy Wright, captain of England, were quoted

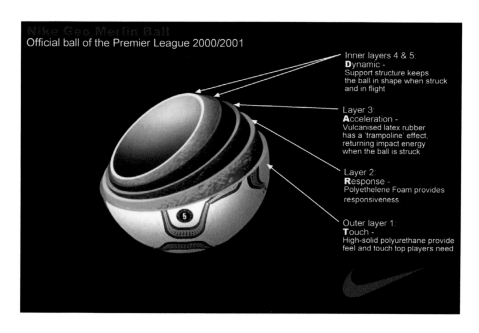

Nike Geo Merlin Ball
Official ball of the Premier League 2000/2001

Inner layers 4 & 5:
Dynamic -
Support structure keeps
the ball in shape when struck
and in flight

Layer 3:
Acceleration -
Vulcanised latex rubber
has a 'trampoline' effect,
returning impact energy
when the ball is struck

Layer 2:
Response -
Polyethelene Foam provides
responsiveness

Outer layer 1:
Touch -
High-solid polyurethane provide
feel and touch top players need

LEFT The latest balls. At the cutting edge of ball technology in 2003 was the very wonderful Nike Geo Merlin Vapor ball.

criticising European slipper-style boots, saying they were more fit for ballet than football. It was considered our players' feet needed to be heavily encased around the ankles, for support and protection. Hungary's devastating 6–3 win over England in 1953 rather indicated that these foreign johnnies might be on to something, not just in their ball technique but in their footwear.

When players slowly began to try out the new slimline boots, made of softer leather and synthetic fibres, they found them more comfortable than the old rock-hard leather boots, and they seemed to help not hinder manoeuvrability. They do of course come off more easily, something you never used to see in former days. Old-style boots came over the ankle, and you laced them round and under your book several times so that your leg was likely to come off before your boot came away.

In 1960, judging by an advertisement in the Southampton programme for a Division Three game against Southend, they were still seen as something of a novelty, as a foreign arrival. 'CONTINENTAL FOOTBALL BOOTS – Introduced to British Clubs by Toomers Sports House, the Football Boot Specialist.'

But by the mid-1960s, the standard British football boot had become lightweight, the same as those used around the world, so there was no need to describe them as Continental. Strangely enough, off the pitch, bovver boots, as favoured by football hooligans, got bigger and heavier, just as football boots got smaller and lighter.

Naturally enough, new ideas, new materials, new amazing scientific advances are still being heralded in football boots and famous players are still being used to promote them. And probably always will.

SHIRTS, SHORTS AND STOCKISTS

The fashion for short shorts also came from Europe and South America. They were at their shortest ever in the 1970s, when players like Glenn Hoddle and Kevin Keegan seemed to be all naked thighs and no shorts at all. What would Lord Kinnaird have made of them? They have dropped a bit in recent years, coming down nearer the knee, but are unlikely to get as baggy and enormous as they were when Alex James was mesmerising the crowds at Arsenal. Numbered shirts, to help identification of players, as introduced in the 1920s by Herbert Chapman at Arsenal, were slow to get official blessing. The first FA Cup Final where they appeared was in 1933. Everton numbered their players 1 to 11, from goalie to left-winger, while Manchester City were numbered 12 to 22, from outside left to goalkeeper.

When they became standard for league games in the 1938–9 season, each team numbered itself from 1 to 11. This led to the general assumption

RIGHT Inside this dainty boot, known apparently as the Air Zoom Total 90, is the delicate but highly expensive foot of Rio Ferdinand.

OPPOSITE Yes, Glenn Hoddle did wear shorts in the 1970s, but sometimes so short they were simply a suggestion of shorts, merely a hint.

among players and spectators that the number referred to the exact position on the pitch. For example that a number 11 was always a left-winger. It was one of the causes, so it was claimed at the time, for England's 1953 thumping by Hungary. England's centre half, Harry Johnson, set out to mark Hungary's number 9, as usual, as he had been brought up to do. But their number 9, Hidegkuti, was not operating as a centre forward, but in midfield, leaving Johnson totally confused.

Names on the back of shirts came in with the Premiership in 1993, and numbers at last ceased to have much meaning positionally once players were allocated squad numbers – going up as high as 50. Notionally, the numbers 1 to 11 still give some indication of a manager's first choice of his best eleven at the beginning of each season, often roughly in their traditional positions, but this can not be relied upon. It is further complicated by some players having favourite numbers, which they insist on, thinking it will bring them luck. Footballers, in this modern age, are still convinced by omens, charms and what they think are good-luck signs.

LEFT Chelsea Megastore. Every club now has a club shop, some more mega than others, selling essential supplies to the fans.

WORLD CUP

JULY 11 to 30
1966
ENGLAND

The Rise of Modern Merchandising

13

AT THE BEGINNING of the 1970s, British football was still relatively untouched by merchandising. Clubs were proud of their pure image, untainted by commercial connections. Football was taking money from the football pools, but that was about the only way they had given in to Mammon. Shirts and stadiums were pure and virgin, rarely displaying any other commercial names but their own. Club shops hardly existed. Supporters wore and waved club scarves, but did not yet wear repro shirts.

OPPOSITE The 1966 World Cup, held in England, saw the first wave of mass merchandising of football souvenirs, covering everything from crisps to clothes, beers to balloons. Fortunately, not all of them featured World Cup Willie.

THE ARRIVAL OF THE MATCH-DAY MAGAZINE

Programmes continued, but paper rationing during the last war meant that programmes, which had been anything up to 24 pages in the late 1930s, were reduced to a couple of pages. This carried on after the war, during the late 1940s and 1950s, and programmes did not recover their size or content for almost another 20 years.

Many programmes from the 1950s look at least 20 to 30 years older than they were, with ancient typefaces, archaic illustrations, showing little imagination or any attempt to sell themselves. Nottingham Forest, like many clubs, just shoved an advertisement on the front, in this case for the local Co-op, as did Charlton Athletic. Neither had a football scene or football content on the cover, so a stranger, picking it up, might not realise it was a programme for a football match. The Charlton cover has at least some social interest, containing a line you never see today. 'Red and White cigarettes – for the man who inhales.'

It's hard to explain why 1950s and early 1960s programmes were so poor when attendances had been booming, creating records all round, with enormous captive audiences eager to read about their teams. One reason was the residue of wartime austerities, but the other was a lack of commercial awareness amongst post-war club directors and a lack of real interest or concern for their long-suffering supporters. Many of these directors were sons or grandsons of the local businessmen who had run the clubs pre-war, in the 1920s and 1930s, who had inherited their shares, but who turned out to be more traditional and less enterprising than their forebears.

When I was writing *The Glory Game* in 1972, a book about a year in the life of Tottenham Hotspur, I was astounded by the fact that Spurs were deliberately turning away money, refusing all advertisements in their programmes, which of course was one reason why they were so thin and flimsy, and even refusing to have any advertising boards inside the ground. Their attitude was that Spurs was a superior club, pure and unsullied, and had no need to stoop to nasty money-making methods. Arsenal, Chelsea and West Ham directors felt much the same.

Out in the provinces, things had already begun to change, and the commercial potentials of programmes and other products had begun to be realised. One of the first to revolutionise their programmes was Coventry City in the 1960s, under the dynamic management of Jimmy Hill. Their previously simple and traditional programme was turned into more of a lifestyle magazine called *The Sky Blue News* with 24 pages, lots of features and photographs of players' wives or female fan-club secretaries wearing surprisingly short skirts – an early example of football and girls being linked together, something which lads mags later capitalised on.

The Sky Blue News was offered as a match magazine, rather than a programme, and in the early issues you can see the arrival and increasing importance of the club's other commercial interests, such as the Sky Blue Bingo and Sky Blue Pool.

In the list of club officials in the April 4, 1970 programme for their game against Stoke City, after the names of the directors and management staff, they included 'Maitre D'Hotel – Giovanni'. An early attempt to make going to the game an eating experience.

From a design point of view, West Bromwich Albion were also pioneers. In 1969, they too changed their format, calling their programme *Albion News*, turning the magazine on its side and employing a graphic designer to come up with some new style of lettering and create a very modern look. They also began to expand their features. In the 1970s they had a women's page and a round-up of records.

ALBION

24.08.02
£2.50

PREMIERSHIP 2002.2003
vS LEEDS UNITED K.0 5.30PM

BARCLAYCARD PREMIERSHIP

ASSOCIATE MATCHSPONSOR ▤ANDYFREIGHT LIMITED▤

MATCHSPONSOR
1ST RESPONSE FINANCE

MATCHBALLSPONSOR
ROGER HOWELL

PROGRAMMESPONSOR
❊ BANK OF SCOTLAND
BUSINESS BANKING

BACK TO**BASICS**
PRE-SEASON IS THE TIME WHEN THE BACK-
ROOM BOYS COME INTO THEIR OWN - WE
INTERVIEW ALBION'S NO.2 FRANK BURROWS

MATCH**ACTION**
RE-LIVE OUR FIRST DAY IN THE PREMIERSHIP
WITH AN 8 PAGE ACTION SPECIAL FROM
OLD TRAFFORD

SIGURDSSON
ICELANDIC WARRIOR LARUS SIGURDSSON, A
MAN WHO TAKES NO PRISONERS TALKS TO US
ABOUT HIS OWN ANGELS & DEVILS!

01

WEST BROMWICH ALBION OFFICIAL MATCHDAY MAGAZINE 2002.2003 WWW.WBA.CO.UK

LEFT West Brom got into the Premiership, at long last, for the 2002–3 season, and for their opening home game on August 24, 2002, against Leeds United produced the first known 100-page programme.

By the 1980s, almost all programmes had changed, some of them becoming little more than extended merchandising catalogues filled with advertisements, most of them either from sponsors or pushing the club's own products. At the same time, they did increase in size and go full colour, with more to read and some excellent action photographs. They also shot up in price. The FA got away with charging £5 for their 1993 FA Cup Final programme. It contained a hologram on the cover, no doubt expensive to produce, but the price was a record for any ordinary programme.

The first ever 100-page programme for an ordinary league match, as far as I can discover, was achieved by West Brom on August 24, 2002, for their first home game in the Premiership. It was a pretty solid publication, with lots to read, and quite a bargain at £2.50.

The modernisation of programmes from the 1970s onwards went hand in hand with the appointment of a new breed of football officials –

promotions managers whose job it was to create or attract other ways of making money for the club, apart from through the turnstile.

THE ERA OF THE PROMOTIONS MANAGER

Club goods had existed for many years, but usually provided by the supporters' club. In the 1930s, supporters could buy various items in their clubs colours, like scarves, rattles, rosettes, cigarette lighters, for men and for women. They had continued after the war. In 1967, Derby County supporters' club were offering club ties in silk for 18/6, and also club badges. By then, such goods were considered rather naff, bought and worn by elderly supporters. The supporters' club passed on any profits to the club itself, who were usually totally ungrateful, continuing to treat supporters' clubs as hangers-on, as they'd always done.

When promotions managers were created at first, their job was to control such goods, such spin-offs, and make sure all the proceeds, if any,

RIGHT Derby County supporters, hiding behind their rosettes.

benefited the club. Their efforts were fairly modest at first, looking for firms and individuals to help with sponsoring the match ball or individual team players.

I contributed myself in 1988, going wild and throwing some of my money away, just to help my home-town club Carlisle United, then in Division Four. I agreed to 'Sponsor a Blue' for a season. The rate was £25 for his strip, £25 for his tracksuit, £25 for his boots and £25 for his training kit – or you could sponsor all four items for the bargain price of £90. Which I did. You then got allocated a player from the first-team pool and every time he played your name went after his in the programme, as his sponsor. I got allocated someone called Gary Fulbrook. He got injured almost at once, or dropped, something happened anyway so that he, unfortunately, never played again, and I only ever saw his name, and my name, in one programme.

Sponsorship made a massive leap into the stratosphere when it moved on from sponsoring the ball or individual players – suddenly you could sponsor whole leagues, or whole competitions, for real money, not just a few quid. In 1970, the Football League was offered a £600,000 sponsorship deal for its League Cup. It turned it down. Several clubs in Europe had already been playing in shirts bearing the name of a sponsor, but the notion of sponsorship had not yet reached England.

The breakthrough, of a sort, came in 1975, when non-league Kettering became the first English club to play a game in sponsored shirts – and the FA told them not to do it again. How disgusting. Certainly not. Go away and wash your shirt out.

But then in 1979 a major club decided to sign a sponsored shirt deal – Liverpool, of all clubs, our heroes, who had made an agreement with Hitachi. Some other clubs followed suit, but TV companies vetoed their use, refusing to transmit games where players could be seen displaying the names of businesses that had not paid the TV companies for the publicity, insisting they must wear blank shirts. This soon became a pretty pointless exercise when almost all clubs were playing all the time in sponsored shirts.

In 1982, the Football League itself gave in to sponsorship when it changed its name to the Canon Football League for the next three years. *Today* newspaper, now long gone, followed as sponsor for a brief period. After that came Barclays Bank, Endsleigh Insurance, the Nationwide Building Society, all sponsors of the Football League, while the League

RIGHT Liverpool in 1979 were the first big club to sell out the soul of their shirts to a sponsor, as Kenny Dalglish demonstrates.

Cup, in its various incarnations, has been called the Milk Cup, the Littlewoods Cup, the Rumbelows Cup, the Coca-Cola Cup and the Worthington Cup. It's now hard to keep up with them, or remember the names which went before. When the Premier League began in 1992, it was sponsored by, can you remember, take it slowly, yes, Carling.

The arrival of sponsorship, meaning commercial enterprises paying for the privilege of being associated with football, getting their names on artefacts which football supporters had always held as precious, such as shirts, stadia and competitions, led naturally to the appearance of a treasured, hallowed, valuable name or emblem on, well, any old rubbish really, as long as money could be made.

In England, the first wave of modern exploitation began with World Cup Willie in 1966. In the past, as we know, there had been football-related souvenirs, such as cigarette cards, postcards, cuff links, plates, ornaments and toys, but mostly produced unofficially, without permission or payments to the clubs or players who were portrayed. The FA now needed the money, so they argued, in order to stage and promote the World Cup games in England, and so charged a licence fee for World Cup Willie and their logo to appear on so-called official goods.

The range of goods on which World Cup Willie appeared was astonishing, when you consider it was the first time we had been exposed to such an onslaught. They included crisps, clothes, dolls, scarves, hats, horse brasses, bed clothes, cigars, cake decorations, beers, braces, belts, masks, dartboards, balloons. There was even an official World Cup Willie song, plus a march and waltz.

This has been the way ever since, for clubs as well as the FA and Football League to licence their names, bringing in billions of pounds in image or copyright fees. In 2002, at the European Court, Arsenal won the right to stop a street trader outside their ground using the Arsenal logo on goods without their permission.

TELEVISION TAKES CHARGE

A vital part of football merchandising, and in fact a vital part of the whole football industry today, is television. Without it, and all the money swilling and slopping around because of it, football would never have developed in quite the same way during the last 30 years or so.

LEFT Cups and competitions have also sold their names to the highest bidders. Ruud Gullit, as manager of Chelsea in 1998, holds up the Littlewoods Cup.

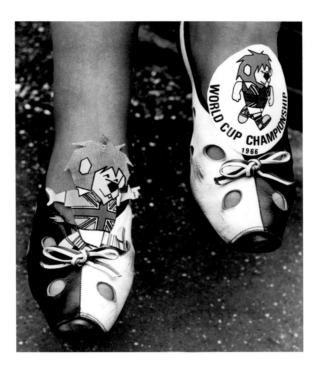

LEFT World Cup souvenir shoes worn by a female fan apparently not at all bothered by the thought of World Cup Willie hovering on her lower leg.

The first radio broadcast of a football match was in 1927 for a First Division game between Arsenal and Sheffield United. Not a lot of people tuned in as there were at the time only 2 million people with a BBC license. In order to help listeners understand what was going on, the *Radio Times* printed a drawing of a pitch divided up into eight numbered segments. One commentator described the play while another commentator called out the number of the squares. This is the origin, it is said, of the phrase 'back to square one'.

The Football League was very wary of this new development, fearing gates would go down, and in 1931, banned live radio broadcasts of league games. When covering an Arsenal game, the BBC, in order to get round the Football League's ban, would arrange for a relay of runners to rush out of Highbury every 15 minutes, arriving breathlessly with the latest news of the game to tell a commentator, crouching over a microphone.

The FA tended to be more cooperative. In 1930, the FA Cup Final was covered live on radio, with the front page of the *Radio Times* being devoted to a plan of Wembley, divided into sections.

Football on film is surprisingly ancient, the oldest known clip being four minutes of a game between Blackburn and West Brom at Ewood Park in

1898. A slightly longer excerpt exists of a 1910 game at Old Trafford. Both clips can be seen at the National Football Museum in Preston. Football became a popular subject for the newsreels shown in cinemas along with the main feature. There was great competition between the rival companies for exclusive rights to big games. During the 1923 FA Cup Final, one company without the rights managed to make a pirate film, concealing their camera inside a giant hammer. Clever trick, and not spotted, because of course the Hammers were taking part.

LEFT Walsall secretary Ernest Wilson entertains the crowd at their old Fellows Park ground in 1952 by playing some of the very latest hit records.

The first football match to be shown on TV was a film of the Arsenal v Everton game in 1936. In 1937, London TV viewers were treated to Arsenal against Arsenal reserves. In 1938, part of the FA Cup Final was shown.

During the 1950s, the FA Cup Final began to be shown live each year, and treated as something of national importance, but the Football League was still reluctant to allow live league games to be covered. Regular football on TV did not begin till BBC's *Match of the Day* in 1964, which showed highlights of the main games on Saturday evenings. Only 75,000 watched the first programme, but by the early 1970s over 12 million were regularly tuning in, over ten times as many as attended games in the flesh. The programme itself, and its signature tune, became a national event.

The arrival of commercial TV led to competition with the BBC to buy rights to football games – at long last the football authorities woke up to the fact that they were sitting on a gold mine. It took them a while to realise what was happening, and how they could turn it to their advantage.

RIGHT The cameras of Sky TV, now a familiar element at Premiership games. Football is currently receiving £1.6 billion over three years for allowing TV to cover matches.

The arrival of satellite TV, in the form of Sky TV, brought on to the scene a TV company whose whole marketing and sales strategy was based on securing exclusive access to the top football games – and so the mad spiral began of enormous sums being offered for TV rights to football. It led to the creation of the Premier League in 1992 when the top clubs decided to break away and retain the main share of the TV revenue for themselves. It was the first major change in the structure of the football administration for over one hundred years, since the arrival of the Football League in 1888.

In 1992, Sky paid £190 million for the rights to Premier League games for five years, and in 1997 renewed its option for four years for £670 million. In 2001, they paid £1.1 billion for three years. Football also got money from other companies, bringing their total TV income to £1.6 billion over three years.

This gigantic inflow of TV money into football, from Sky, the BBC and other broadcasting companies, totally revolutionised football, making the leading clubs incredibly wealthy, enabling them to charge even more for sponsorship rights and marketing deals, all because of the TV exposure. And this time, unlike ye olden days, when players got little from the big gates and nothing from football pools money, they made sure they got their share. Footballers were suddenly able to become millionaires. Who would have expected that, back in the years of post-war austerity.

ABOVE Cigarette cards, which were free as long as you bought a packet of fags, have long gone, but football stickers can still be bought and collected. They did big business during the 2002 World Cup.

Post-War Players, Fame and Money

14

THE MOST FAMOUS post-war player was Stanley Matthews, the Wizard of Dribble, though he had been a star player before the war, having first played for Stoke City aged 17 in 1932. After the war he joined Blackpool, helping them to three Wembley finals, but it was not until 1953, the 'Matthews Final', that he won a cup winners' medal. He moved back to Stoke in 1961 and played with them till 1965, playing his last game on February 6, 1965, against Fulham – at the age of 50 years and five days. Hard to imagine any professional ever playing to that age again.

He was knighted in 1965, while still a professional, another record more than likely to remain unbroken, and was the first professional footballer ever to be so honoured. The first knighthoods for football had been awarded to administrators many years earlier – to Sir Charles Clegg of the FA in 1927, Sir Frederick Wall in 1930 and Sir Stanley Rous in 1949. Footballers, active or otherwise, were a long way from being considered worthy of such honours.

Matthews, a slightly built winger who with a shrug of his shoulders was able to confound every defender and thrill the crowds, deserved it in every way. He was a pure winger, a creature who does not exist any more, now that work-rate, tracking back and defending are deemed so important. He was known for his healthy lifestyle, which no doubt contributed to his long career – and he was never once booked or sent off.

Billy Wright, captain of Wolves and England in the 1950s, was also never booked or sent off, which in some ways is more remarkable than Matthews achievement, given that Wright played centre half. He was the golden boy of his age, admired by all, and not just for his golden curls. His influence and his wavy hairstyle can be seen in photographs of the Wolves team of 1949.

OPPOSITE Stanley Matthews, will we ever see his like again? Others have had flashes of his famous body swerve while hugging the right wing, but few, if any, will get near the length of his career. He played professional football from 1932, aged 17, until 1965, aged 50.

All his fellow players seem to be copying his haircut, but then footballers have always been easily influenced.

Billy Wright, like Tommy Lawton and Tom Finney, or Willie Waddell and George Young in Scotland, and other post-war stars, didn't have the money of present-day players, but Wright was about the first to be seen as having a glamorous lifestyle, part of showbusiness, after his marriage to Joy Beverley, one of the singing Beverley Sisters. Before the war, and just after it, footballers did not move in such exciting circles.

Bobby Moore was a hero, and golden haired, and for captaining England's World Cup team in 1966 was loved by a grateful nation, but as a defender he was more solid than exciting.

The first player to be seen by the general public as glamorous in his own right, exciting and even sexy, was George Best of Manchester United, hailed for his looks, his hair, his style almost as much as for his football skills. Several other 1960s and 1970s players such as Rodney Marsh managed to create a similar image, if not quite the same female following, with their fast cars and their fashionable clothes.

GROWN MEN KISSING ...

Out on the pitch, there came an interesting sea change around the 1960s. Players had always congratulated each other on a goal, usually giving thumbs-up, and there are old photos in which players can clearly be seen shaking hands, but mostly they returned demurely to their positions.

It's hard to date exactly when cuddling and kissing came in. There were isolated spottings in the 1970s, when it still was deemed to be a nasty Italian or South American habit that could not catch on over here. Real men did not touch each other or show emotion in such a way. The FA were very worried that some of our players might pick up this rather disgusting foreign habit, and in 1976 the FA's match committee suggested that players who kissed and cuddled after a goal was scored should be charged with bringing the game into disrepute. Fortunately, for once, the FA showed some common sense and rejected the idea as impractical.

In 1981, FIFA's technical committee expressed concern that goal celebrations were getting out of hand. They felt it was all right for the goalscorer to be congratulated by the team captain, or the person who had made the final pass, but when the whole team jumped on top of the scorer, smothering him in kisses, desperate to embrace him, this was going a bit far and held up the game, and they recommended that the national associations should curb this habit forthwith. Some attempts were made, with players being penalised for taking off their shirts, running behind the goal or into the crowds, but celebrating in some way after a goal is very hard to eliminate.

Had not Lord Kinnaird in 1882 stood on his head, a celebratory ritual which for some reason never quite caught on?

By the 1990s, real men, even in Britain, were showing real emotions, even in public. In 1990, we had the sight of Paul Gascoigne in tears during the World Cup. By then, kissing and cuddling had became the norm. Close-up shots on TV even showed some players doing mouth-to-mouth kissing. Players were quoted as saying that scoring a goal was better than sex, providing the same sort of climax, so it was natural they might want to cry out in delight and ecstasy.

By the time of the 2002 World Cup, it was clear that many teams and players had worked out special celebratory rituals – special movements, either for amusement or political significance. There had also arisen the habit of pulling up one's shirt in celebration to reveal a white t-shirt with a message written on it, even if it was just 'Joy and Love and Jesus'.

LEFT Players had always congratulated each other on a goal, and there are old photographs in which they can be clearly seen touching hands, but mostly they returned demurely to their positions. Now kissing is the norm, as R. Ferdinand and D. Beckham demonstrate.

HAIR WE GO ...

From the beginning, players were concerned about their clothes and their hair styles. In the late 1920s, for about a decade, a middle parting was deemd appropriate. In the 1930s, the more fashionable had wavy hair, swept high. After the war, Brylcream kept things slick. In the 1970s and 1980s, Kevin Keegan and Bryan Robson had notable perms. Since the 1990s, David Beckham, right, seems to have had a different hair style every season, sometimes every game.

It has been rare for a whole team to adopt exactly the same hair style at the same time, but this was what the Romanian team did during the 1998 World Cup, emerging with all eleven players, their hair newly bleached.

MORE MONEY AND TOO MUCH JEWELLERY

The first breed of managers to appear glamorous was in the late 1970s and early 1980s with the arrival on the scene of Ron Atkinson, John Bond and Malcolm Allison. They became known for their jewellery and coiffured hair, for drinking champagne and wearing flash clothes, the sort of image which contrasted sharply with the older generation of managers who had actually won things, such as Bill Shankly of Liverpool or Bill Nicholson at Spurs.

By the 1960s and 1970s, more money appeared to be coming into football, judging by the better lifestyles of the better-known players and managers compared with their pre-war equivalents, but in reality, money in football had hardly arrived. Players were still roughly earning little more than two or three times the average of the skilled worker.

RIGHT AND OPPOSITE And then in the 1980s, managers became stylish and glamorous, or at least like Ron Atkinson, they started wearing jewellery sun glasses and worked hard on their tan, or puffed on a big cigar like Malcolm Allison.

The maximum wage for professional footballers continued after the war at £8 a week, as it had been since 1922, despite the record-breaking crowds. Admission fees were admittedly relatively low, still only one shilling, but with 40 million going through the turnstiles in the late 1940s the clubs could easily have rewarded the players better. The players' union threatened strike action, but all they got was a slightly higher off-season rate. In 1951, the maximum did creep up to £14 a week and then in 1958 it rose to £20 a week.

Star footballers of course had always been able to earn a little bit on the side, which got greater over the years. In 1951, Stanley Matthews was receiving £20 a week from the Co-op for the use of his name. It doubled his football wage, so probably seemed a good deal at the time. Denis Compton promoted Brylcream and put his name to annuals and articles. Arthur Rowe in 1957 had his name on a pair of boots which were widely advertised.

Things got better for players when the maximum wage was finally abolished in 1961, after a long battle led by the Professional Footballer's Association chairman Jimmy Hill, and a successful court action by George Eastham, who accused his former club Newcastle United of restraint of trade by not allowing him to move to a club of his choice, in his case Arsenal, when his contract had expired. The battle went to the High Court, which ruled in his favour.

These two events signalled the end of almost one hundred years of players being little more than hired hands, with no freedom of movement and heavily restricted earnings. The PFA liked to believe it was the end of 'football slavery'. It did not make an enormous or immediate difference to the conditions and wages of most players (that had to wait until the TV money of the 1990s), but 1961 can be seen as the beginning of the modern era. British players from then on were able to take charge of their lives and maximise their incomes.

As soon as the £20 maximum was abolished, Tommy Trinder, chairman of Fulham, announced that Johnny Haynes was the first £100-a-week footballer in Britain. Haynes had already been making a few extra bob through his star status. In a Fulham programme for 1960, he was recommending the Wembley Vinyl Ball as the world's best vinyl ball. His big pay rise at Fulham was a move to stop him being tempted abroad.

There had been a flurry of players going abroad – mainly to Italy where they had already been managing to pay what seemed like sky high wages, at least double what was on offer here.

John Charles had led the way, going to Juventus in 1957 for £70,000, receiving a £10,000 signing-on fee and £60 a week in basic wages. In the 1960–1 season, he was followed by four of our best players: Joe Baker went from Hibs to Turin for £73,000, Denis Law from Manchester City to Turin for £80,000, and Aston Villa's Gerry Hitchens to Inter Milan for £80,000.

Jimmy Greaves came back to England in November 1961, just after the abolition of the £20 maximum wage. Bill Nicholson paid £99,999 for him, not wishing Spurs to be the first British club to pay £100,000 for a player. It is noticeable in Greaves's contract with Spurs, which has only recently been made public, that his basic wage was still £20 a week, though he did get £4,000 as his share of the transfer fee. In that contract, you can still see the power that clubs had over their players. Clause 5 for example stated 'that the player shall not engage in any business or live in any place which the Directors of the club may deem unsuitable'. He also had to 'do everything necessary to get and keep himself in the best possible condition so as to render the most efficient service to the Club'. Which was fine, in theory, till later on Jimmy's drinking habits made him less than efficient.

TRANSFER-FEE INFLATION

Transfer fees between British clubs had risen steadily since the war. In 1947, Tommy Lawton went from Chelsea to Notts County for £20,000. In 1960, Denis Law went from Huddersfield to Manchester City for £50,000. In 1966, Alan Ball broke the British £100,000 barrier going from Blackpool

LEFT In 2002, Rio Ferdinand moved from Leeds United to Manchester United for £30 million, making him Britain's most expensive player and the world's most expensive defender.

to Everton. The £200,000 mark was reached when Martin Peters went from West Ham to Spurs in 1970. In 1979, David Mills went from Middlesbrough to West Brom for £500,000. The £1,000,000 mark was finally broken in 1979 when Trevor Francis went from Birmingham City to Nottingham Forest.

Once the million-pound mark was reached, it quickly jumped into multiple millions. In 1996, Alan Shearer went from Blackburn Rovers to Newcastle United for £15 million. In 2002, Manchester United paid £30 million for Rio Ferdinand from Leeds, making him Britain's most expensive player and the world's most expensive defender, though not the world's most expensive transfer, which in 2003 was still the £46.5 million paid by Real Madrid for Zinedine Zidane.

Players' wages however did not at first shoot up at the same rates or along the same curve as transfers. In the 1960s and 1970s, star players in star clubs, despite winning lots of pots and lots of glory, did not earn huge amounts. The normal wage in the mid-1970s for a First Division player was around £200 a week.

I recently asked Bobby Charlton what he earned at the height of his playing career. His best year was in 1968, by which time he was a World Cup winner and European Cup winner. Yet in that year, all he earned was £15,000. Which is about what a current Manchester United star earns in one day.

George Best did better, but then he was a glamorous player. He tells me that in his best years at United he was making around £30,000 a year – but half of that came from advertising and sponsorship. Once he retired, his income dropped dramatically.

Today, however, he has benefited from a new and interesting trend – the cult of the famous footballer. In 2003, aged 56, he was earning far more money than he ever earned in his twenties when he was playing. By becoming an icon, a legend in his own time and later, turning out endless versions of his life story, he was able to make a substantial amount of money from publishers, newspapers, TV and advertising.

Alan Hansen, the ex-Liverpool player, has revealed that when he retired in 1991 his average wage was £1,500 a week, which now seems pathetically low, for a top footballer. It indicates that the wage spiral did not really rise dramatically till the mid-1990s, after the combination of increased TV and sponsorship revenue and the Bosman ruling of 1996, whereby players who were out of contract could leave a club for nothing and negotiate their own financial arrangements. Naturally, if their new club did not have to pay a transfer fee they were more likely to offer greatly increased wages. Which they did. From 1996 onwards, players wages increased at around 30 per cent each year.

In 2003, the average Premiership player is reckoned to be earning £10,000–15,000 a week from football. They all have agents, plus lawyers and other advisors. When their commercial interests are added in, they are *all* capable of easily earning £1 million a year. Even Alf Common would never have believed it.

Black Players

15

ONE OF THE OTHER STRIKING FEATURES about football in Britain today, which would be a surprise to all football fans of the post-war years, is the number of black players. We think of it as a purely modern development, but as with most things in football, it can be traced back to its beginnings.

It has been recently claimed that Britain's first black player was Andrew Watson, who turned out for Queen's Park in 1874 and also toured with the Corinthians in 1884. Not much is known about him, except that he was born in Georgetown, British Guyana, educated in Halifax in Yorkshire, and trained as an engineer. The Scottish Football Museum, whose director Ged O'Brien maintains that football as we know it really, really began in Scotland, not in the English public schools, is keen to prove that Watson was the first black player, albeit an amateur.

ARTHUR WHARTON AND WALTER TULL ... THE PIONEERS

It is still generally agreed, however, that the first black professional footballer was Arthur Wharton, who joined Preston North End in 1886. He was technically then still an amateur, but in 1889 he signed professional forms for Rotherham Town. There has been a biography (written by Phil Vasili in 1998) and also a TV documentary, part of modern day research into the history of black players in Britain, which has revealed that there were more in the past than anyone ever realised.

By 'more', it probably means around ten players with a black or mixed-race background out of a total of some ten thousand who played football for a British league club between the 1880s and 1914. Most of them played for lower League clubs, and not for long, and their precise ethnic backgrounds and footballing histories have disappeared or been written out of the records.

OPPOSITE Arthur Wharton, England's first black professional footballer. Started as a professional sprinter, then became goalkeeper for Preston North End in 1886. He later moved to Rotherham and Sheffield United. This is a studio portrait of him which appeared in a book called *Famous Footballers*, an indication of how well known he was in his day.

RIGHT Andrew Watson, back row centre, who played for Queen's Park of Glasgow in 1874 – now claimed to be the first British black player, but always as an amateur. Research is still going on into his background and playing career.

The interest in and knowledge about Arthur Wharton is partly because he played for a famous club, Preston, who became known as the Invincibles, and also because of his middle-class, educated background. He was born in Ghana, the son of the Revd Henry Wharton, a Methodist missionary who had originally come from Grenada in the West Indies. Arthur came to England to train at a college for Methodists, intending to become a missionary, moving into professional football after success as a professional sprinter. He had no more than two seasons with Preston and does not appear to have played for them during their Invincibles season of 1888–9 when the league began, according to the teams printed in my *Sporting Chronicles*. During that season, if not before, he had moved on to Rotherham. He later played for Sheffield United in the First Division, then Stockport County till 1902, so he had a good career in football which lasted almost 20 seasons.

Wharton was a goalkeeper, and became known for what many goalkeepers have become known for being a bit eccentric, not to say daft as a brush. Many years after he had finished playing, in a letter to a Sheffield newspaper, a spectator remembered one of Wharton's more entertaining moments. 'In a match between Rotherham and Wednesday, I saw Wharton jump, take hold of the crossbar, catch the ball between his legs and cause three onrushing forwards to fall into the net. I have never seen a similar save since and I have been watching football for over fifty years.'

All experts at the time were not convinced by his skills, according to a writer in 1887 in the *Athletic Journal*. 'Good judges say that if Wharton keeps goal for North End in their English Cup tie, the odds will be considerably lengthened against them. I am of the same opinion ... Is the darkie's pate too thick for it to dawn upon him that between the post is no place for a sky lark? By some it's called coolness – bosh!'

Wharton's skin colour was often drawn attention to in the press – but then so was Dixie Dean's – but contemporary match reports do not mention if he was picked on or racially abused by spectators. He ran a pub when he retired, and then became a colliery worker, dying in 1930.

The next black player of note to play in the top division was Walter Tull. His grandfather had been a slave in Barbados, but his father came to Folkestone, in England, worked as a joiner and married an Englishwoman. She died young, the children were put into care, and Walter grew up in an orphanage. He played for Clapton and then was signed by Spurs in 1909, who had just got into the First Division, going with them on a pre-season tour of Argentina and Uruguay. He played for Spurs for two season, during which he was racially abused at an away match at Bristol City. They were 'Bristol hooligans,' so a report described them, 'who made a cowardly attack upon him in language lower than Billingsgate.'

In 1911, Tull was transferred to Northampton Town. During the First World War, he was called up and, amazingly, became an officer, the first black officer in the British army – amazing because military codes at the time were against officers of colour, stating that white soldiers would never take orders from them at the front. Tull became a second lieutenant – and was killed on the Somme in 1918.

In the 1920s and 1930s, there were a handful of black players, none playing with a leading club, the most notable being Eddie Parris, an outside left with Second Division Bradford Park Avenue, who in 1930 was capped by Wales.

In South America, part of Uruguay's early success was due to the fact that there was no colour bar imposed on their players, and their team was multiracial – unlike Brazil's. In 1921, the president of Brazil banned black players from the national team in the South American championships. Slavery in Brazil had ended only in 1888 and there were still deep social and racial divisions in the country. Some of the Brazilian league clubs did have black players, which often led to disagreements when other clubs refused to play them, while those of mixed race would try to lighten their face with rice powder before taking the field. By the 1930s, the barriers had been broken with black players becoming the stars and folk heroes of Brazil.

ALBERT JOHANNESON OF LEEDS

In England, after the last war, there was a trickle of black players who had come from South Africa, the most famous and successful being Albert Johanneson, who joined Leeds in 1961. He was a winger yet became their top scorer in the 1963–4 season and played in the 1965 FA Cup Final, the first black player to do so. It was felt, however, that he never quite fulfilled his potential. He was abused on the pitch by other players, being called a black bastard, to which Don Revie, the Leeds manager, told him to respond by calling them white bastards. He was also singled out, being a tricky winger, for physical abuse, which he found hard to cope with. He took to drink and drugs and died aged 53 in poverty, back in South Africa in 1992.

There have been enough white players, especially clever ball players, before and since, who have given in to drink and other temptations, but what was held against him, and came for a while to represent a stereotype of black players in the minds of white coaches, was that he didn't have the 'bottle'.

For a generation, this held back the chances of black players in English football. When I was researching *The Glory Game* in the early 1970s, I came across many football coaches who insisted black players would never make it here. They wouldn't survive the winters, so it was believed, hated muddy pitches, didn't like it up 'em, couldn't dish it out, and were generally softies, fancy dans who chickened out.

There wasn't a lot of logic in this myth, especially when the other stereotype of black athletes at the time was that they were muscle-bound, fast, fearsome. It was also the case by then that the young black players coming through were British, had been born and bred here, spoke Cockney or Brummie, were well used to our horrible winters. Yet older football coaches still retained this prejudice against them.

CLYDE IS BEST FOR HAMMERS

The mass arrivals from the West Indies had begun in the 1950s, invited over to help out our workforce, and were soon providing a small but steady stream of British-born, second-generation black players. But the one who attracted all the attention, and who is now considered among the first modern-day black players to succeed in the First Division, was Clyde Best.

Best was not British born but arrived here in 1968 as a 17-year-old from Bermuda, having been offered a trial by West Ham. It's a wonder he didn't turn straight round and go home. There was no one to meet him at Heathrow, he got off the Tube at the wrong station, West Ham's ground was closed when he got there, and he wandered around and got lost till fortunately a stranger directed him to a council house where another 'coloured' West Ham player, Clive Charles, was living.

I interviewed Clyde Best in the same house three years later in 1971, while he was still living there with Mrs Charles, his landlady, who was in fact white. By this time Clyde was a star of the West Ham first team, scoring magnificent goals, terrorising defences up and down the country. Imagine a Premier League star today living in a council house. It was his skills which attracted all the attention, many football fans believing he was the first black player to play here, forgetting about Johanneson and never knowing about Wharton and Tull.

What struck me most about him was his politeness and shyness. He didn't drink, didn't go out on the town – though he had recently been led astray by two older players, Jimmy Greaves and Bobby Moore, and fined for being out late in a club at Blackpool.

He was experiencing racial abuse at several away grounds, but seemed to be coping. His problem, if he had a problem, was that he appeared too gentle, not always making the most of his 6ft 1in and 13 stone. As with Emile Heskey later on, he got criticised by some being fans not for his colour but for apparently not being ruthless enough.

Clyde Best appeared 186 times for West Ham between 1969 and 1975, scored 47 goals, then left for Feyenoord in Holland, later disappearing to the United States.

By chance, when visiting Bermuda in 2001, I met him again, as he turned out to be living round the corner from my hotel. He had come back to Bermuda from California, where he'd run his own cleaning firm, to coach the Bermuda national side. He'd left that position and was now working in a

prison. He was enormous, appearing to be well over 20 stone. 'Don't ask. It's not nice.' But he looked fit enough, no longer shy and quiet, but out going and affable.

He had no regrets about his football career, nor the fact that he made so little money. While at West Ham, he was earning only £8,000 a year. 'They're in show business now, so they should get paid like TV or film stars. I think they deserve it.' The only thing he'd wished he'd done was swap some shirts with Bobby Moore, or that he'd kept more of his own football artefacts. He'd just been reading about the enormous prices now being paid in Britain for football memorabilia, which he could hardly believe.

'When I played in England, I did get a lot of hate letters, terrible things, abuse on and off the pitch. Other players did say awful things to me, but not all. Bobby Charlton always had a nice word for me, and people like Bob Wilson and Paddy Crerand. They were good people. I just tried to tell myself that not everyone is going to like you in this life, for whatever reason. With the ones who called me names, I tried to make them silly by putting the ball through their legs and beating them.

'All black people got abuse in those days. People forget it now. Nurses and teachers from the West Indies, they had to put up with it. I was alone at the time in football, the only black player in the First Division. My dad told me to stick it out, ignore the abuse. He said I owed it to everyone to make a go of it. I remember him saying, "It's not for you, it's for all the people after you."'

BRITISH-BORN BLACK FOOTBALLERS

After Clyde Best departed, the tide of young, British-born black players finally broke through. In 1977, Laurie Cunningham got into the England Under-21 team, the first black player to wear an England shirt, then in 1978, Viv Anderson of Nottingham Forest made it into the full England team. In 1978, Cyrille Regis was voted Young Player of the Year by his PFA colleagues. John Barnes's wonder goal against Brazil in 1984 made all English fans rave about one of our boys doing well, without having to mention or even think about his colour. But during the 1980s and early 1990s there was still appalling racial abuse at many grounds, which the football and other authorities tried hard to stamp out.

Between 1987 and 1997, the number of black players in league football doubled. Today, around 15 per cent of our professional footballers are black

OPPOSITE Clyde Best who was born in Bermuda and played for West Ham in the 1970s, was seen at the first of the modern-day black footballers in first-class football, but there were others, long before him, who had been forgotten.

and it is now uncommon to see any side without at least one black player. In
the England team, and in the Arsenal team, they are often in the majority,
outnumbering the white players.

Black stars can be loved or hated, jeered at or applauded, called names
like Fatty or Ugly, like any other player, without their colour coming into it.
It was noticeable that when Sol Campbell left Spurs in 2002 for Arsenal,
arousing incredible fury and abuse from Spurs fans for being disloyal, I
never heard people shouting that he was a black bastard. Just a common or
garden bastard. Though there were also sexual taunts, just to annoy. So has
racial prejudice gone from the British game? Not quite, alas. There are still
rightwing elements stirring it up for their own political ends and also
ignorant fans reacting blindly, without thinking.

Shaka Hislop, the Trinidad-born goalkeeper, in writing the foreword to
a book about the history of black players (*Colouring Over the White Line*
by Phil Vasili), recounts an incident in 1996 when he was playing for
Newcastle United.

'I was at a petrol station opposite St James' Park when a group of around
six kids, no more than 12-years-old, began shouting racist abuse at me,

calling me every name under the sun. Then one of them recognised me. "hey, that's Shaka Hislop." They all came running over and asked for my autograph. My initial reaction was one of amazement, then I was utterly dumbfounded. Without saying a word, I quickly got into my car and drove off ...'

LEFT After Clyde Best departed, the tide of young, British-born black players finally broke through. In 1977, Laurie Cunningham got into the England Under-21 team.

Foreign Play and
Foreign Players

16

BRITAIN EXPORTED FOOTBALL around the world, and it is in the nature of things which go around the world to come back, sometimes in different forms, sometimes to haunt you. It was a bit of a shock in the 1950s to have to agree that many of the pupils abroad were now playing football better than the masters here at home. And in the 1990s, there came another surprise when we found them not just content with playing it over there, in their own countries, but migrating over here, stealing our game and the hearts of our fans and our women, infiltrating all our famous clubs. In the case of Chelsea, it has recently happened that every Chelsea player on the pitch has been a foreigner. How did it all come about?

Football was exported at a time when we were exporting everything. As the home of the Industrial Revolution, our goods, capital, services and skills, workers and pastimes went round the world. We had an empire, were still a dominant power in the world, which meant sending out colonial administrators to vast tracks of the globe still painted red.

At home, the propagation of football had been twofold, the amateur, well bred, public-school chaps eventually handing it over to the horny handed, cloth-capped workers. When it spread abroad, there were two similar sources of insemination. The officer class set up social and sporting clubs when they found themselves in some far-flung corner, regardless of the heat or the local conditions and traditions, in order to carry on life as they had lived it at home. Hence so many of the oldest football clubs in Europe and South America owe their origins to British expats, and even sometimes their present-day names. At the same time, ordinary British sailors and soldiers, railway workers and industrial labourers, when they fetched up on a foreign shore, started a kickaround which eventually grew into a team.

In the history of many of the older overseas football clubs there can also be detected a third element, spreading the seeds of football. When middle-class students came here from abroad to polish off their education and learn some English, they often took football back with them, starting clubs at home.

BRITISH INFLUENCE

The earliest foreign football clubs took root in Denmark and Holland and in France in the 1870s. France's oldest club, Le Havre, was formed in 1872 after a game against visiting British sailors. In Switzerland, the game was imported by British boys at local finishing schools. The main Swiss club was originally called Lausanne Football and Cricket Club. There are still Swiss clubs with English names such as Grasshoppers of Zurich and Old Boys of Basle. In Italy, local British residents in 1892 began the Genoa Cricket and Football Club and in 1898 the Milan Cricket and Football Club, later called AC Milan. Milan, meaning the football club, is still spelled in the English manner, not Milano. In Spain, football was first introduced in 1893 by British workers in Bilbao. In Scandinavia, football was first planted by Scottish shipyard workers.

In almost every European country there was a British connection, direct or indirect, the earliest clubs being formed by a combination of British residents and middle-class locals who had studied in England. And it all happened very quickly, almost as soon as the FA and the Football League had knocked the laws and the leagues into shape. An explanation for the speed could be that there had already been a tradition of folk football, as in Britain, with different versions of kicking a ball towards some sort of goal going back centuries. Once someone somewhere formalised the rules, it wasn't, therefore, too hard to join in.

In South America, it caught on just as quickly as in Europe, with football clubs being formed as early as the 1890s. The first Uruguayan team was created by an English professor at Montevideo University while it was British railway workers who formed Uruguay's first sporting club in 1891. Uruguay became the most football mad of the South American countries, though Argentina can claim the oldest British sporting club, formed in 1865, while Brazil first tasted football when the Royal Navy made a visit in 1884. These three countries are still the heart of football mania in South America, with many of their league clubs retaining vestiges of their English names, such as Old Boys, Racing Club, Juniors, Corinthians.

One of the energising agents in the early growth of football abroad was that even from the early years of league football in Britain, British teams went on foreign tours, flying the flag, spreading the word – or just swanning off in the summer to have a good time. Corinthians, as we know, played 23 matches in South Africa in 1897. In 1898, Queen's Park from Glasgow were touring Scandinavia. In 1904, Southampton became the first professional English team to play in South America.

In return, overseas teams came here on tours, such as the Canadians who were playing in England in 1888, the year the Football League began, with the *Sporting Chronicle* reporting on their games. Which brings us to a slight anomaly, ruining some of the theories about how Brits came to spread football round the world. If Britain was so dominant, football so infectious, why is it that in so many English-speaking nations with a mainly white population and imperial connections, like Australia, Canada, New Zealand and the USA, that football did not end up as their major game? One reason is that they had created and established their own ball games with their own rules and did not want to ape the pastimes of the colonial masters. There were different circumstances in each country. Meanwhile, football boomed in Europe and South America, unfussed by colonial connections.

FIFA AND THE BRITS

FIFA, the world body of football, was created in 1904 by seven of the European countries where football had first flourished: France, Belgium, Denmark, Holland, Spain, Sweden and Switzerland. The football authorities in England, Scotland, Wales and Ireland refused to take part. They did eventually join, then left again in 1920. They were back in 1924, leaving again in 1928.

There were various specific disagreements, over things like payments to amateurs, but the basic problem was inbred superiority, a belief that it was our game, so no one else was going to tell us how to play it. 'I don't care a brass farthing about the improvement of the game in France, Belgium, Austria or Germany,' said Charles Sutcliffe, a member of both the FA and the Football League in 1928. 'The FIFA does not appeal to me. An organisation where such football associations as those of Uruguay and Paraguay, Brazil and Egypt, Bohemia and Pan Russia, are co-equal with England, Scotland, Wales and Ireland seems to me to be a case of magnifying the midgets ...'

So the first World Cup in 1930 went ahead without any of the British countries. Only four European countries made the long sea journey to Uruguay: France, Belgium, Romania and Yugoslavia. The King of Romania picked his country's team and managed to get each of them off work so they could travel abroad. All four countries went on the same boat, which took two weeks to reach Uruguay with the players exercising on the decks to keep fit. On board was Jules Rimet, the French lawyer who was president of the FIFA, carrying the World Cup trophy in his luggage.

Uruguay was a suitable host for the first World Cup, having won gold for football at the previous two Olympics in 1924 and 1928. It was also celebrating the centenary of its independence in 1930. Thirteen countries in all entered, Uruguay beating Argentina 4–2 in the final.

England finally agreed to rejoin FIFA in 1946, in time for the first World Cup held after the war, in 1950 in Brazil, and suffered the ignominy of

ABOVE Uruguay training for the 1930 World Cup. Uruguay had won gold for football at the the 1924 and 1928 Olympics.

being beaten 1–0 by the USA in the first round. We knew by then that certain European nations had been progressing well at football, but not the baseball-playing Yanks. That was a shock.

MOSCOW DYNAMO

One of my earliest memories of foreign footballers, while still at primary school, was hearing about Moscow Dynamo when they came here on a short tour just after the war in 1945. It all seemed so exotic, these stocky, well drilled footballers who didn't even speak English, yet could play the game so well. I cut out their photographs from the papers and stuck them in my scrap book, along with my favourite Scottish players. They attracted massive crowds – 82,000 at Stamford Bridge against Chelsea, 90,000 at Ibrox to watch them against Rangers – and received plaudits from the

ABOVE Uruguay scoring another goal during the 1930 World Cup Final. Uruguay won the trophy.

RIGHT One of my earliest memories of foreign footballers, while still at primary school, was hearing about Moscow Dynamo when they came here on a short tour just after the war in 1945. This is them in 1936.

experts and polite applause from the crowds. They were partly exhibition games, so we didn't get too alarmed. Not till the 1953 drubbing of England by Hungary in a proper international. That's when we all finally realised that funny foreigners could teach us a thing or two about our game.

Those foreign players all went back home, to Russia or Hungary, none of them being signed by any of our British clubs. Which is what would have happened today.

BELOW Two players with foreign blood who became well known footballers in the 1930s – Frank Soo of Stoke City and Berry Nieuwenhuys, known as Nivvy, of Liverpool.

FRANK SOO
Stoke City F.C.

THIS SURFACE IS ADHESIVE . ASK YOUR
TOBACCONIST FOR THE ATTRACTIVE
ALBUM (PRICE ONE PENNY) SPECIALLY
PREPARED TO HOLD THE COMPLETE SERIES

ASSOCIATION
FOOTBALLERS
A SERIES OF 50

37
B. NIEUWENHUYS
(Liverpool)

A South African international born
at Kroonstad, Orange Free State,
Berry Nieuwenhuys (known to the
crowd as "Nivvy") was invited to
join Liverpool and he signed on as a
professional in season 1933/34. Almost
at once he was a big success as out-
side-right, showing exceptional speed
and shooting power with either foot.
He is also extremely good in heading.
As a South African he is qualified to
play for England and his form is up
to international standard. "Nivvy,"
who is an enthusiastic motorist,
speaks Dutch as well as English.
He stands 5 ft. 11 in. and weighs
11 st. 8 lb.

W. D. & H. O. WILLS
MANUFACTURERS OF GOLD FLAKE, CAPSTAN,
WOODBINE AND STAR CIGARETTES
BRANCH OF THE IMPERIAL TOBACCO CO.
(OF GREAT BRITAIN & IRELAND), LTD.

B. NIEUWENHUYS (LIVERPOOL)

FOREIGN STARS ... FROM ARDILES TO ZOLA

It's hard to decide who was the first foreign player to play over here. Depends of course what you mean by foreign. They could have a foreign background, with a foreign-sounding name, like Frank Soo of Stoke City in the 1930s, but have been brought up here, which often happened. It was much rarer for a foreign player, playing abroad, to get transferred here. Until the 1950s, the mentality of British managers and coaches worked against such a thing, believing foreigners couldn't play properly, but it did happen now and again.

The earliest known foreign players include a German, M. Seeburg, an inside forward who played for Chelsea, Spurs, Burnley, Grimsby and Reading between 1907 and 1914; an Egyptian called H. Hegazi, centre forward for Fulham in 1911–12; an Italian, A. Freezie, a half-back for Reading in 1913–14; and a Dane called Nils Middleboe who played left-half for Chelsea in 1913–14. Middleboe was a Danish international and had a successful career at Chelsea, playing 46 games.

Not many foreign players got washed up on these shore in the 1920s and 1930s, and in fact the FA made sure it was unlikely to happen, imposing a residential qualification in 1931 which lasted till 1976, requiring professional players to have lived in the UK for at least two years. South Africans found it easier, being part of the empire, and several did well, such as Berry Nieuwenhuys, who signed professional forms for Liverpool in 1933. His name was a bit of a mouthful, so fans called him Nivvy.

One or two foreigners did appear after the last war, hang on and get a few games, the most notable being Bert Trautman, an ex-German prisoner of war in England, which might not have been all that pleasant but it did give him residency. He was Manchester City's well-loved, well-regarded goalkeeper between 1949 and 1956 and helped them win the FA Cup in 1956, despite playing with a broken neck. At the end of that season he was voted Footballer of the Year, the first foreigner to have the honour.

The modern-day wave of foreign players, a wave which is now a flood, is generally agreed to have started with the arrival in 1978 of Ossie Ardiles and Ricardo Villa at Spurs. Ardiles had been a vital part of Argentina's

LEFT Bert Trautman, ex-German prisoner of war, who helped Manchester City win the 1956 FA Cup, despite playing with a broken neck.

World Cup-winning team, and Villa had played twice as a sub. It was expected that if they went anywhere they would go to a Spanish or Italian club, with cultural and linguistic connections, bigger wages and better weather. Until then, there had been no tradition at all of South Americans playing in Britain.

Manager Keith Burkenshaw had flown out to Argentina, just two weeks after their World Cup success, and signed both players for a combined fee of £700,000. Spurs had just returned to the First Division, so felt they had to do something to show seriousness of intent and add a bit of excitement and glamour. Around 10,000 fans turned up to see them train at the pre-season open day. The press considered it a ground-breaking move, buying

not just one but two foreign players, and of such proven quality. 'It was as if
the janitor,' reported the *Guardian,* 'had gone off to buy a tin of paint and
come back with a Velasquez.'

I went to see them in their first league match, away against Nottingham
Forest, for *The Sunday Times,* who gave my report the headline 'Vamos
Vamos Boys'. Villa got Spurs' goal, in a 1–1 draw, but it was Ardiles who
most impressed, with his intelligence, cunning, directness. One of the Spurs
players told me afterwards about their effect. 'It's made everyone that bit
more competitive. Nobody wants to look a mug in front of the new lads.'

Villa stayed only a few seasons, but his Cup Final replay goal of 1981
against Manchester City will, you can be sure, be shown again and again
down the years. Ardiles played for Spurs for nine years, taking a diplomatic
break in Europe during the Falklands War, but returned, still loved by all
Spurs fans, and went on to become manager. His name lives on in song at
Tot-ing-ham (as he pronounced it), thanks to 'Ossie's Dream'.

Ardiles was unusual for English football in being from a middle-class
background, the son of a lawyer and halfway through his own legal training
when he took up professional football. He could speak good English, as well
as being a good player. Later players from abroad did not always integrate
quite as well or stay as long, but the success of Ardiles at Spurs and of the

Dutchmen Arnold Muhren and Frans Thijssen at Ipswich, who brought elegance and the 1981 Uefa Cup to Portman Road, did much to encourage the purchase of other foreign players.

By the 1990s, the trickle had become a stream, and soon they were regularly winning Player of the Years awards, as Eric Cantona of Manchester United did in 1994 and 1996. He remains a cult figure, his name still sung by the fans long after his retirement. Jürgen Klinsmann, a German and reputedly a 'diver', both of which might have been held against him in earlier years, was also well loved by Spurs fans. At Arsenal, their fans for several years have been singing 'There's only one Dennis Bergkamp', while at Chelsea Zola has become one of their favourite players. In 2003, Zola was even voted 'the greatest player in the club's history'. These four foreigners, and others, proved just as popular as the homegrown heroes of earlier years, such as Dixie Dean or Denis Law. Bergkamp, by the way, got his Christian name from Law, but his father chose to spell it differently, an example of the cross-fertilisation among present day football fans.

BOSMAN AND THE MODERN ERA

The Bosman ruling of 1995 made the arrival of foreign players much easier, at least for Europeans from European Community Countries, as did their relative cheapness, especially that of players from Eastern and Central Europe, whose names might not have been well known in Britain but who were considered better value than similarly priced English players.

The sudden wealth of the Premier League in the early 1990s meant that at first the imports were either cheap unknowns or international stars coming towards the end of their careers, but soon clubs like Manchester United were able to pay vast sums for foreign players at the height of their careers, such as £28 million for Juan Sebastian Veron and £19 million for Ruud van Nistelrooy.

Some people in football, such as the players' union, regretted the influx of foreign players, arguing that it was stifling the development of homegrown players now, unable to get into their first teams, while romantics moaned that foreign mercenaries were ruining the English and Scottish games. Rangers and Celtic too became predominantly foreign teams. They longed for the so-called good old days when English teams fielded English players, citing the classic example of West Ham. Their 1965 European Cup-winning team, like their 1964 FA Cup-winning team, was not only all

English, without even a Scotsman or Irishman, but they were mostly local lads, brought up in East London or nearby Essex.

It's an idle fantasy, of course, to expect that an English league team named after an English town or district should consist of players entirely drawn from that particular area. It won't ever happen again. And it never

RIGHT Many players have won Best Player of the Years awards, as Eric Cantona of Manchester United did in 1994 and 1996.

really happened in the past. Ever since football became professional in 1888, players have been mercenaries, willing to move anywhere and at any time if the money is good enough.

In 1901, when Spurs of the Southern League won the FA Cup, guess how many of their 11 players came from London? Or from the South of England? The answer is none. There were five Scots, two Welshmen, one Irishman. Of the three English men, one was from Maryport in Cumberland, one from the Potteries and one from Grantham.

For over a century, the 'foreign' element in every English team came from Scotland, with enough Scots in most clubs to play England against Scotland in training matches. Now, alas, the supply of good players from Scotland seems to have dried up – for reasons no one has adequately explained. Perhaps the pendulum will swing back one day.

There are compensations, of course. The influx of so many top foreign players and foreign managers, most of whom have high skills, good attitudes, intelligence, discipline and good healthy habits, has had a beneficial effect on the Premier League, greatly increasing its quality for those of us watching and also improving the skills and lifestyles of the British-bred players, or at least those who manage to get in the teams.

There's another by-product of all these foreign imports. In the 2002 World Cup, there were 68 foreign players playing for their national teams who were currently earning their living in Britain – nine Swedes, nine Danes, eight Frenchmen, six Americans, four from Cameroon, four from Turkey, three from Croatia, three from South Africa, three from Slovenia, two from Germany, two from Equador, two from China, two from Argentina, two from Japan and one from Belgium.

All these 68 foreign players were well known back in Britain by the followers of their respective British clubs. There will doubtless be an equally high proportion of British-based players performing in the European Championship of 2004 and the World Cup of 2006. So in international competitions to come, when England, Scotland, Wales and Ireland get eliminated, the chances are that we will always have players to follow. I was at Highbury in February 2003, watching Arsenal play Ajax of Amsterdam, and heard Arsenal fans cheering on 'Paddy' and 'Bobby'. At first I thought they might be new signings, then I realised they meant Patrick Vieira and Robert Pires. It was a sign not just of affection for these French players, but an attempt to anglicise their names, making them one of us.

Women Players

17

WOMEN IN FOOTBALL has happened only recently, that's probably what most men think today, still not having quite got used to seeing women playing football live on TV, reading reports by women on the sports pages, having them sounding knowledgeable on radio and TV football programmes, listening to them arguing down the pub, or looking along the rows of seats at football matches and seeing, yes, quite a few women fans, and thinking, Hmm, far more than I remember when I was a lad.

FEMALE FACE IN THE CROWD

If you peer closely at random crowd scenes from pre-war football games you will in fact see quite a few female faces. They were always there, even if not in great numbers. In a report of the Queen's Park v Wanderers game at Hampden Park in Glasgow in 1875, it said that '4,000 spectators turned up, including many ladies.' The players were of course gents at the time, so naturally would attract some ladies. But working-class women also turned up when working-class men started to take part, and some of them were quite well organised. For the FA Cup Final of 1905, a group of female followers of Newcastle United, calling themselves the 'Newcastle Ladies Final Outing Club', arranged their own trip to London, much to the surprise, and only a slight degree of scorn, of a male newspaper commentator. 'They had their own lady secretary, paid their own subscriptions and with the latter day independence of the sex, came to London in their own saloon, without the assistance or company of a single mere male.'

In a 1907 Chelsea programme, there's a reference to the existence of young female supporters. 'A wonderfully quiet crowd, with a consideration that allows the girl or small boy to take up a position in front of a tall man.'

OPPOSITE Miss Nettie J. Honeyball, secretary and captain of the British Ladies Football Club in 1895. She wanted ladies to play the man's game, but show it could be womanly.

In 1948, according to a Manchester United players brochure, the team had four very loyal, and very pretty looking young female supporters, complete with scarves and rosettes, who made one of the biggest sacrifices anyone could make for their team at the time. 'The United Four', said the caption to their photograph, '... are invariably to be seen at our games and pool their sweet ration to provide chewing-gum for the boys.'

As for playing, we know that women were the first of the species to be seen mucking around with a ball, according to Homer, while the first evidence I can find of an actual women's football match occurred in 1881 in Edinburgh, reported in a local newspaper.

'So it has come at last! What next? Two teams of women have just played a game under Association rules in Edinburgh. Several years ago there was a rage for silly displays of certain kinds of athletics by women, but we thought the time had passed for another outburst in the form of Association Football ... The football shown was of the most primitive order. It is said that other matches are to come off, one in Glasgow this afternoon. If it does ... it will most probably be on some of the professional running grounds. No football

BELOW Women supporters exisited from the beginning, although there were few of them. In 1948, these four Manchester United fans made the final sacrifice for their heroes, according to a Manchester United souvenir brochure isssued for the 1948 FA Cup Final.

Here we have United's other mascots, the United Four.   They are invariably to be seen at our games, and pool their sweet ration to provide chewing-gum for the boys.

club with any regard for its good name would encourage such a humiliating spectacle made of the popular winter pastime ...'

The writer was clearly aghast at the very notion of women playing football, dismissing it as silly, but it is interesting that he should then go on to suggest some sort of active boycott, as if he personally had been humiliated or was perhaps fearful it might actually catch on. This seems to have been a common feeling among football's male officials, though they did little about it at first.

LADIES OF LONDON DON THEIR BOOTS

In 1895, the British Ladies Football Club was formed in London. They organised their first game on March 23, 1895, at Crouch End Athletic's ground, between teams from North and South. The President was Lady Florence Dixie, youngest daughter of the Marquess of Queensberry and said to be the first female war correspondent. The secretary and captain of the club was Miss Nettie J. Honeyball whose address was given on the poster advertising the game. She invited 'ladies desirous of joining the club' to write to her. Miss Honeyball, a name which should really be in a James Bond film, was quoted in the newspapers as saying that she wanted girls to play 'a manly game and show that it could be womanly as well'.

Miss Honeyball played for the North team – presumably meaning North London, as opposed to North of England. She and the other players wore what look like very heavy, long-sleeved blouses, possibly made of canvas, baggy knickerbockers, boots and rather formidable-looking shin-guards, worn on the outside over their socks in the style of male players. Over ten thousand spectators turned up, paying one shilling each. The British Ladies Club must therefore have made a few bob, as there is no suggestion on the poster that the game was for charity.

Ladies teams spread to other parts of the country, and their clothes are always drawn attention to in any newspaper report, which suggest that many men were there to gape and gawp and perhaps giggle at the sight of females running around rather than actually watch the football. A few years later, women moved into male shorts and football tops, showing quite a bit of bare knee. Women players took their football seriously, just as they did the sport of riding bicycles, part of a movement for more freedom and independence and power for women as desired by the suffragettes.

THE LADY PLAYER

The fellows are anxious, it would seem,
To have a game with the ladies team.

LEFT Despite what a 1900 postcard might say, men in football, especially officials, wanted to keep women in their place.

But men in football, especially officials, wanted women kept in their place. Even someone apparently as enlightened, educated and athletically gifted as C. B. Fry, writing in *CB Fry's Magazine* in 1905, was against it. 'The idea of a girl playing ball as in the famous picture of the Greek ladies on the marble terrace is absolutely delightful. The idea of a girl playing football is grotesque.'

In *Association Football and the Men who Made It* by Gibson and Pickford, published in 1905, volume three, a writer on London football was still appalled at what had happened at Crouch End, ten years earlier. 'A phase of metropolitan football that was distasteful in the extreme to all who had the well-being of the game at heart was the "enterprise" that led to the appearance of "Lady Footballers". They played at Crouch End before a 10,000 gate in 1895 and, thank heaven! they subsequently became as extinct as the dodo, so far as the Metropolis was concerned. The whole thing was farcical, if not worse!' So farewell the British Ladies Football Club, at least in London. They would appear to have had an upper-class, moneyed element, just as male football had done in its early stages. But then, as with the men's game, ordinary, working women folk took it up, for reasons that could not have been expected.

DICK KERR LADIES

In 1914, when the First World War broke out, over 1 million women went to work in munitions factories, replacing men sent off to the front. This sudden social and sexual upheaval lead to many women forming their own factory football teams, especially in the North of England. In 1916, the *Barrow Guardian* reported a game between Ulverston Munitions Girls and Ulverston Athletic, the munitionettes winning 11–5. Similar games were noted in Manchester, Liverpool and Tyneside – but what became the best known women's team sprang up in Preston: Dick Kerr Ladies.

When I first heard of them, I presumed there was a man called Dick Kerr. In fact there were two. W. B. Dick and John Kerr, who were founders of a large factory in Preston which made tramways and railway equipment. They moved into munitions when the war began and took on women workers. In October 1917, with so many men away, the factory's football team was not doing so well, which led to light jeering and mockery by some of the women. 'Huh, call yourself a football team, we could do better.'

LEFT The redoubtable Dick Kerr Ladies of Preston went on to break every possible record for a women's game in Britain when in 1920 they played before a crowd of 53,000 at Goodison Park.

It began when some women joined in a kickaround with the apprentices in their dinner break and led to them organising their own team to play on a nearby field. The women's team did surprisingly well, being young and fit, and they also enjoyed it. At Christmas that year, they were asked to help support a local military hospital and decided to play a game against another women's team from a local foundry, with the proceeds going to the hospital. They hired Deepdale, home of Preston North End, for a fee of £5, and on Christmas Day afternoon, 1917, 10,000 people turned up to watch the game – no doubt many of them already feeling pretty jolly after their Christmas dinner. The large sum of £600 was handed over to help wounded soldiers.

It had been such a success that Dick Kerr Ladies went on to play games against women's teams from Lancaster, Bolton, Barrow and Whitehaven, drawing equally good crowds and making a lot of money for charity. They were doing proper training by now, had their own manager, a draughtsman from the factory called Alfred Frankland, and were winning almost all their games. Deepdale officials were happy to let out their ground, as they sold lots of refreshments, and the management at Dick Kerr were pleased by all the publicity.

As they got better and played more matches, they did what professional teams did – started signing up any good talent they spotted, usually from one of the teams they had played against. A likely girl would be visited at her home by the manager and tempted away – offered a job at Dick Kerr's factory, plus a place in the team and fixed up with local digs. The girls were almost all young and single, and quite enjoyed the adventure. Officially, they were not being paid for playing football, but received expenses and a sum to make up for their loss of working hours, which usually came to around ten shillings a game.

From Lancashire and the North-West, they started moving further afield, playing a game at St James' Park, Newcastle, against Newcastle Ladies in March 1919 which attracted a crowd of 35,000. Although the war had finished, the girls carried on playing. The charitable needs were just as great, with so many war wounded returning home. In the 1918–19 season, they played some 30 games all over the North.

It is estimated that by 1920, there were 150 women's teams all over the country, many of them like the Dick Kerr Ladies with their origins in wartime factories. They had also sprung up in France. In April 1920, Dick

Kerr invited over the French Ladies Football Team to play four games against them in England – at Preston, Stockport, Manchester and London. The game at Deepdale drew a crowd of 25,000, while in London, at Chelsea's Stamford Bridge, there were 10,000 spectators.

Dick Kerr then made their own French tour in October 1920, attracting crowds of 23,000 in Paris and between 10,000 and 16,000 elsewhere. Back in Preston in December they played a match by floodlight at Deepdale, getting special permission from the Secretary of State for War, Winston Churchill, to use two anti-aircraft searchlights. They provided excellent light, except when an operator turned his searchlight right into the faces of some of the girls, temporarily blinding them. Over 10,000 turned up, including dozens of pressmen and the cameras of Pathé News.

On December 26, 1920, Dick Kerr's Ladies broke every possible record for a women's game in Britain, then or since, when at Everton's ground in Liverpool, Goodison Park, they beat St Helen's Ladies 4–0 before a crowd of 53,000. Over £3,000 was raised for charity by this one game – a sum

BELOW England Ladies, as represented by Dick Kerr, played France Ladies in 1920, and naturally started off with a kiss.

equivalent to £250,000 today. In June, 1921, they played Bath Ladies at Manchester United's Old Trafford and got a crowd of 35,000.

During 1921, the girls played 67 games watched by a total of 900,000. The games were all for charity, mostly played at league grounds before enthusiastic supporters. Some might have come along to gawp and giggle in the early days, and the games were often billed as 'Holiday Entertainment' but most people were impressed by the skill and speed of the female players. Such huge crowds would hardly have continued if the only attraction had been the novelty.

A measure of the success and acceptance of women's football was the arrival of magazine stories based round a woman player. In 1921, the popular weekly *Football and Sports Favourite* was serialising a story called 'Nell O'Newcastle' about Nell Harmer, 'a very pretty girl and a clever footballer', who worked at a Tyneside engineering concern. There was also on sale a 'grand, long and complete sports novel' entitled *Meg Foster – Footballer.*

Mr Frankland, Dick Kerr's manager, proved an efficient organiser and highly disciplined, not letting his girls wear trousers in public while travelling with the team, making sure they trained hard and played hard, did not bring the game into disrepute and kept out of the pubs, though one or two of the girls were fond of a beer or two on the coach home.

FA BANS WOMEN'S GAME

And then came the bombshell. On December 5, 1921, the FA unanimously decided to outlaw the women's game. They banned any club associated with the FA from henceforth letting them use their ground. Their objections were twofold.

'Complaints having been made as to football being played by women, the council feel impelled to express their strong opinion that the game of football is quite unsuitable for females and ought not to be encouraged.

'Complaints have also been made as to the conditions under which some of these matches have been arranged and the appropriation of receipts to other than charitable objects.'

The names of complainants were not given, nor any evidence to support the allegations. The health risk to women had been long debated, with medical experts being divided – some saying it harmed women's bodies, making them incapable of giving birth. Other doctors said it kept them healthy. If fit young women could work in factories, they could certainly play football. After all, they played hockey with sticks. 'Football is no more likely to cause injuries to women than a heavy day's washing,' Dr Mary Lowry was quoted in the *Lancashire Daily Post* after watching a game.

The suggestion of financial fiddles, that too much money was going on so-called 'expenses', was never properly investigated, which is what the FA should have done and stopped any further abuses, instead of coming down so heavy-handedly. Fiddling around with the money in football had been done from the beginning, with under-counter payments, pounds in socks, help with the house moving and other inducements resulting in gate receipts not always quite tallying with the stated size of the crowd.

But had there been financial corruption? Gail Newsham, who wrote a book about Dick Kerr's ladies in 1997 *In a League of their Own*, seems to think that Mr Frankland had personally done very well out of the team, managing to buy his own business, but gives few facts. He maintained that in four years he had handed over £50,000 to charities. The girls were still on their ten bob a game, and there's no suggestion that they were in on any scam. They also all admired and liked Mr Frankland and remembering him later had nothing but praise for him. Very likely, he did no more than normal football clubs did – covered up payments they did not want officially revealed, all for the good of the club, or so they would say.

The women themselves, and all women footballers everywhere, ridiculed the financial and medical slurs put about by the FA. They believed that the real reason for the ban was jealousy. The women were attracting bigger crowds than many of the male clubs, and doing so much for charity, unlike the men. The FA couldn't stand the competition, said the women, seeing their game as a threat to male pride and power, as if they were being mocked by women playing their game, and so they turned nasty and spiteful, imposing a ban.

There was an attempt by the women to administer themselves through the creation of their own Ladies Football Association but having no proper football grounds to play on was a serious handicap. Almost at a stroke, the FA had killed off the women's game. Most women's clubs gave up.

But Dick Kerr Ladies continued. They were supported by a big firm and they were able to hire rugby grounds and running tracks. Even when all the men had returned to their factory jobs, Mr Frankland managed to fix them up with jobs in a local hospital. In 1922, they sailed off for a three-month tour of Canada and the USA. The Canadian part of the tour was a bit of a shambles, as the English FA managed to lean on the Canadian FA to cancel games, but in the USA the women attracted crowds of up to 10,000 – playing against men's teams.

In the 1930s, and now calling themselves Preston Ladies, they had celebrities like George Formby, Gracie Fields and Joe Loss to kick off their charity games. In 1937 in Edinburgh, they played against a Scottish women's team to decide who were the women's world Champions. They won 5–1, but only 1,000 turned up, nothing like the crowds of 1922. After the Second World War, with crowds coming back to football generally, they managed 5,000 for a game at Glossop.

The FA kept up its disapproval of women's football, even banning a referee from officiating at league games because he had trained a team of Kent ladies. In 1957, Mr Frankland died, aged 75, and the club never really recovered. It finally packed up in 1965 when they ran out of players. During a period covering almost 50 years, they had played 828 games, winning 758 of them, had attended 160 civic receptions and contributed £175,000 to charities. Not many football clubs, male or female, can boast such a record.

ABOVE. There was still some prejudice around about ladies playing football, and a lot of cheap jokes.

BAN LIFTED BUT PREJUDICE REMAINS

The year after Dick Kerr Ladies disbanded, England won the World Cup and there was an upsurge in people playing football, including women. In 1969, the Women's Football Association was formed. In 1971 it was recognised by the FA – 50 years after they had banned it.

There was still some prejudice around, and a lot of sneering from some men. Ron Atkinson, known throughout the football world for his way with words, many of them his own, was quoted as saying that a woman's place was either in the kitchen, the disco or the bedroom, not on the pitch.

A magazine called *Football Digest*, in its September 1973 edition, ran a mocking piece about what would happen, now that the FA had recognised women players. 'Dare we anticipate headlines proclaiming the transfer of the dashing centre forward Miss Georgina Better from Manchester Suffragettes to the WI Athletic for £100,000 with the luscious left-half

thrown in as a make-weight.' The writer worried how women would cope when 'chest trapping' the ball and about 'pregnancy and menstrual instability'. He envisaged women players fretting about the colour and design of their shirts, women spectators demanding 'sumptuous armchairs in homely colours', but for male fans it would be good 'bird watching'.

WOMEN'S GAME GOES GLOBAL

In 1993, the FA itself took over the responsibility for women's football in England, which is still the case. In the last ten years, there has been a fourfold increase in the number of women playing football. In 2003, the FA estimated that there are 7,000 women's football teams, playing in leagues affiliated to the FA. When school teams are added in, the total number of women playing football is 500,000. It means that football is now the number one female sport in England, more popular than either hockey or netball.

The growth abroad has been even more remarkable – in Germany, France, Norway and China, and especially in the USA where they hosted the 1999 Women's World Cup. The USA won a final watched by 90,000 and their players became household names, notably Mia Hamm, who was said to be earning £100,000 a year. Football in the US was greatly helped by a law in 1972 which gave girls sports in school equal funding with boys.

In England, Fulham Ladies FC became a full-time professional team in 2001, while half of Arsenal's team were full-time pros, in the sense that they had paid jobs with Arsenal, coaching girls in Arsenal's women's football academy. Fulham and Arsenal met each other in the Women's Cup FA Final of 2001 at Crystal Palace's ground before a crowd of 12,000. Not quite up to Dick Kerr Ladies at their height, but a commendable crowd, considering that women's football in England had hardly existed 30 years earlier. It is expected that half a dozen other women's teams will become fully professional in the next few years. At the top of the pyramid of women's leagues is the Premier League which has three divisions – a national league of ten teams, then north and south divisions of 12 teams each.

The main women's football games in England are now shown live on Sky TV, and the huge box-office success of the film *Bend It Like Beckham* in 2002, which was about an Asian girl wanting to play in a women's team, brought even more women into football.

If the present global rate of expansion continues, FIFA predicts that by 2010 there will be more women than men playing football around the world. Who could ever have predicted that? Certainly not C. B. Fry.

In England, women's football even had its own fanzine, *On the Ball*. I asked its editor, Jennifer O'Neil, who played for Oxford University, while studying geography, and then for Sunderland AFC Women, what she thought were the reasons for the massive increase in women playing football. She suggested one element might be Girl Power: 'Girls now do feel empowered to have a go at anything boys do.'

It might also have something, marginally, to do with football itself becoming more feminine. And I'm not just thinking of David Beckham often dressing and behaving like a girl. In 1921, when the FA banned the women's game, football was indeed very much a man's game. The boots weighed a ton, and so did the ball when wet, the pitches became quagmires

when it rained, goalkeepers got physically assaulted, charged into the net. But today the rules have changed, with no tackling from behind. Players wear slippers as opposed to hobnail boots, on well-drained pitches. Skill and fitness is what matters now, not brawn, so why shouldn't women play it just as well as men? Now, more than ever, football is for all.

LEAGUE COLOURS — TOTTENHAM HOTSPUR · SALFORD · ROTHERHAM COUNTY · HUDDERSFIELD TOWN · HULL KINGSTON ROVERS

LEAGUE COLOURS — NOTTINGHAM FOREST · LEEDS · STOCKPORT COUNTY · STOKE · BRIGHTON & HOVE

LEAGUE COLOURS — KEIGHLEY · MIDDLESBROUGH · ROCHDALE HORNETS · READING · NORTHAMPTON

LEAGUE COLOURS — HUDDERSFIELD · BLACKPOOL · SWANSEA TOWN · WIGAN · WAKEFIELD TRINITY

LEAGUE COLOURS — BIRMINGHAM · LIVERPOOL · WOLVERHAMPTON W. · BOLTON WANDERERS · WARRINGTON

FOOTBALL

Football and the Arts

18

IS FOOTBALL ART? Well, it's scarcely a science, despite what some coaches might think. Is it a craft? Yes, in the sense that you can be put through an apprenticeship, made better. Most people would agree that footballers are born not made, but have inherited a gift which has to be worked on but was always there. Football could be described as art in that it can be artistic, creative, pretty, pleasing to watch and, now and again, has geniuses practising it. In the old days, it was a fleeting art, retained only in the memory of the audience that day. Now it can live on, thanks to the wonder of video. Any activity, any object can be described as a work of art, so by that definition, football is an art. But of course it's not. Football is a game, which now and again can also be beautiful.

FOOTBALL IN FINE ART

Throughout its history football has thrown up items which are works of art, pieces of craft, words of wisdom, objects of value, things to be studied and researched, collected and cared for and displayed. Not all that many, but as we move forward we look back and treasure more what went before.

The best-known football painting of the nineteenth century was painted in 1839, long before football as we know it began, by Thomas Webster RA and exhibited at the Royal Academy (*see* pages 22–23). It shows a rural scene, with some rosy-cheeked village boys chasing after a ball, pushing and shoving, a few of them clutching their heads and legs, having been injured. The ball can be clearly seen – and it appears to be leather, perhaps even with panels. It's a pretty rural image, rather than a football painting, but was no doubt typical of what happened in country places before football as such became organised.

OPPOSITE Peter Blake RA, has created several works with a football element, notably *F for Football* which was a limited screen print in 1991. He was inspired by old cigarette cards and some Baines cards, originally produced in the 1890s.

The best-known football painting of the twentieth century, of football as it was till quite recently, is L. S. Lowry's *Going to the Match* which he did in 1953. It's certainly the most expensive. The painting was bought in 1999 by the Professional Footballers' Association for £2 million. The setting seems more like 1933, with the industrial landscape and the open stands and terraces. The ground is not named – you can just see 'Football Club Co Limited' – but is assumed to be Burnden Park, Bolton.

Lowry himself was not a football fan. He was just fascinated by the crowds, seeing football as part of the landscape in which he lived. He painted an earlier one, in 1928, which had the same title and the same sort of spectators in the foreground, but the stadium can't be seen.

Alfred Wainwright, another Northern artist, who wrote and drew the *Pictorial Guides to the Lake District*, was a very keen football fan, following Blackburn Rovers all his life and in 1939 was one of the founders of the Blackburn Rovers Supporters Club, of which he was Hon Treasurer and then Chairman. In 1940 he helped organise a coach trip to Wembley for the War Cup Final against West Ham. He had printed some club postcards, on which he did little drawings, but he never drew a proper football scene.

Peter Blake RA, has done several works with a football element, notably *F for Football*, which he produced as a limited screen print in 1991. Michael Ayrton, Carel Wright, Michael Rothenstein, Alan Lowndes, Paul Nash are other twentieth-century British artists who have now and again painted or been inspired by a football subject, but few of our leading painters have made a study of football, turning out a body of work on the subject.

The FA, to celebrate its 90th anniversary in 1953, in an unusual and enlightened act of sponsorship, organised an exhibition called 'Football and the Fine Arts' in London, to which many leading artists of the day contributed, including L. S. Lowry with his *Going to the Match*. One of those who exhibited was Alfred Daniels with a painting of a match in progress at Fulham. He did an equally excellent football painting in 1969 – I know how excellent it is as I have it hanging on my wall as I write – which shows a group of park footballers, in London I assume, perhaps Hackney Marshes. I like it because it could be anywhere, the sort of Sunday-morning scene familiar to us all.

Abroad, especially France and Italy, many well-known artists of the day have turned their attention to football, but often representationally, rather than realistically, picking on one of the more abstract aspects of football: the flight of the ball, the blur of the tackle, the emotion of scoring. They include Picasso, perhaps the most famous artist of all to have used football as an inspiration. In 1961 he did a study called *Footballeurs* in which some blotchy, amoeba-like footballers are competing to head a ball, but you can clearly see it's a football scene. In the USA, Andy Warhol did a work showing Pele with a ball, but that was more a fashion statement than a piece of art.

ILLUSTRATION AND COMMERCIAL ART

Football illustrations, as opposed to fine art, have a longer history. Football themes can be found in wall carvings, panels, woodcuts, engravings, silk screens from ancient China and Japan and medieval Europe. Or what we take to be football scenes. Some of them were done some time later, imagining what people did, what people played, in the past.

English illustrators and caricaturists, such as Rowlandson in the 1780s and Cruikshank in 1823, were using a football as a means to get across some political point long before the Football League existed. The use of a football, being kicked about, as a political or metaphorical image, in art and language, predate organised football, showing how just how old football is in our culture. Parliamentarians and political writers used the term 'political football' to describe someone or some idea being knocked about from as early as the eighteenth century.

Commercial art, commissioned and completed to deadlines can often be artistic, if not always considered so at the time. The early Baines cards of the 1890s, which preceded cigarette cards, were little works of art in themselves, sold in packets in little shops, showing club colours, slogans and players.

When boys' magazines, comics and boys' annuals started running football stories and serials, many of the drawings were done by professional illustrators, most of them now unknown. The front illustrations were usually in colour, with handsome lettering.

Cartoonists turned their hands to the subject of football almost as soon as football became professional, as can be seen in the pages of *Punch*. The editors of the football pages and football programmes were also very keen on cartoons. In the 1920s and 1930s, most of the front covers of the Chelsea and Spurs programmes had a cartoon, picking up some incident from the last game. With Spurs, they had a running cartoon figure known as

PREVIOUS PAGES A painting showing Sunday morning football by Alfred Daniels in 1969. Daniels was one of the artists who exhibted at the FA's Football and the Fine Arts show in 1953.

RIGHT Baines cards from the 1890s.

Cocky – after the cockerel – while Chelsea's programme had the Pensioner, after the Chelsea Pensioners. Football cartoons were meant of course to be funny rather than artistic.

The most artistic English football programmes were probably the early 1920s FA Cup Final programmes, when they were trying their best to be imposing and impressive, particularly the 1922 Final when they hired the well-known illustrator Bernard Hugh to draw the elaborate cover, which he did in the classical style with columns and a female figure representing Victory (*see* page 231)

Football posters have always been highly artistic, especially for World Cups, notably the 1930, 1954 and 1982 posters, when the best artists were commissioned. Original copies now fetch very high prices. The 1966 World Cup poster, though collected, can hardly be called artistic, showing as it does the ineffably naff World Cup Willie.

Postage stamps have to be considered small works of art. The earliest with football themes were issued by Uruguay in 1924 and then in 1928, to celebrate their victories at football in the Olympic Games. Neither issue featured an actual footballer. The earliest stamp with a footballer, as far as I can find, is a Bulgarian one from 1931. The first World Cup stamps to appear were Italian in 1934, featuring footballers in various poses, which are very attractive, as are the French ones for 1938, the Swedish set for 1958 and, surprisingly, England's World Cup stamps for 1966 which fortunately did not feature Willie.

HISTORY BOOKS, COMICS AND FANZINES

Books and magazines about football, after that first blossoming around 1900, with the fine writing and high-class production and photographs, rather tailed off in the 1920s and 1930s. After the last war, they remained weedy and old-fashioned for a while, thanks to paper restrictions and ancient printing technology. However, one of the post-war developments in this area was the beginning of club histories. Only a handful of clubs had had their official stories published before the war, notably Celtic and Rangers in Scotland and Blackburn Rovers in England. The first history of Manchester United, surprisingly, did not appear till 1946. Since then, there have been around one hundred assorted histories of the Old Trafford club.

LEFT Mr Punch in 1914 was critical of professional footballers still playing after the war had started.

Many of the oldest established clubs celebrated their centenaries in the 1970s and 1980s, which gave them an excuse for official histories to be commissioned, some of them quite handsome. Now all of the 92 League clubs have had at least one club history published, even those who have never won anything.

In recent years, there have been some football biographies such as those by Sir Alex Ferguson and Roy Keane, which have earned at least a million pounds each, thanks partly to newspaper serialisations. But probably the most lucrative football book of all time, in sales and income and film rights, was Nick Hornby's *Fever Pitch*, about his devotion to Arsenal, published in 1992.

Some post-war football comics have acquired cult status, such as early copies of *Striker* and *Roy of the Rovers*. Roy first appeared in *Tiger* magazine in 1954, winning matches for Melchester Rovers and solving international mysteries, doing so well that in 1976 he was promoted to star status with his own magazine *Roy of the Rovers*. He's now dead, killed in a helicopter crash in 1993, but has since passed into the language. Hardly a post-match analysis passes without someone saying, 'It was real *Roy of the Rovers* stuff...'

Football fanzines are a relatively modern development, with no counterparts before the war. Football writing, even at the cheaper end of the market, was on the whole laudatory, not to say fawning, but the advent of cheaper printing methods in the 1980s, often done on kitchen tables by students, or student types, was an encouraging antidote to hooliganism, letting the world see that not all young supporters were in it for the violence, well, not physical violence. Fanzines did offer a critical view of football, often obscene and libellous, attacking their own clubs and players as much as praising them. The origins go back to *Foul* in the 1970s, which was partly based on the *Private Eye* formula, but proved, like Martin Peters, too ahead of its times and folded in 1976. But many of the fanzines which came later, such as *When Saturday Comes*, have continued and grown to become established publications. There are also some glossier, well-produced football magazines, including *Four Four Two*.

SONGS ... FROM THE TERRACES TO THE WEST END

Football and music have gone together ever since the crowds started singing, but usually the crowds have created their own chants and words, pinching a tune from elsewhere. In the 1900s, lots of sheet music was sold with football themes, trying to cash in on the popularity of football. These were often comic songs, mocking the referee.

There hasn't been much about football on the stage, though as early as 1896 there was a four-act musical drama called *The Football King* which

ABOVE Films with a football theme were being made from as early as 1911, but not very successfully. *Gregory's Girl* (1980), however, was a hit, starring John Gordon Sinclair (above).

made the West End. A hundred years later, Arthur Smith's *An Evening with Gary Lineker* also made it to London, after success at the Edinburgh Festival. There hasn't been much of note in between. Since then, Andrew Lloyd Webber and Ben Elton's musical *The Beautiful Game* in 2000 had a football theme, set in Northern Ireland, but was not considered a huge success.

There have been a surprising amount of films with football connections, but unsurprisingly none has been rated highly by film buffs. The first known football feature film was a silent short called *Harry the Footballer* from 1911. *The Arsenal Stadium Mystery* began as a novel then became a film in 1930. Michael Caine starred in a 1981 film called *Escape to Victory* in which Bobby Moore had a walk-on, or at least a kick-in, part. *Bend It Like Beckham* in 2002 and *Gregory's Girl* in 1980 were considered better, more enjoyable, more successful films – and each concerned girls playing football. Now what does that prove?

FROM MEMORABILIA TO ACADEMIA

Football memorabilia came to be considered works of art when the leading
auction houses started regular auctions. The first of note was held by
Christie's in Glasgow in 1989 when a Cup Final medal won by Alex James,
estimated at £1,000, went for £5,000. Today, whoever sold it is probably
kicking him or herself as it must be worth at least ten times that amount.
Now Sotheby's, Christie's and all the leading auction houses have regular
sales. It's impossible to keep up with the latest prices, as records get broken
all the time, but in 2001 Bobby Moore's World Cup-winner's medal was
sold for £150,000, and in 2002 Pele's 1970 World Cup Final shirt went for
£157,000. These, in theory, are unique items, connected to a famous player,
but ordinary items, produced originally in their thousands, now fetch small
fortunes. Football programmes, if they are old and interesting enough, can
go for £10,000. Sets of old cigarette cards, originally free, can be worth
£3,000. So throw nothing away. It's been estimated that if a regular football
fan now in his seventies had kept every programme and ticket for every
match he'd been to since the war, he could sell them for £20,000 – and get
more than all his money back.

If you can't afford to buy or bid for historic or interesting football stuff,
then you can visit some of the football museums which are now springing
up all over the country. In 2003, there were seven proper football museums,

LEFT Major auction houses,
such as Sotheby's and
Christie's, have had sales of
football memorabilia
since 1989. Some treasures
from a Sotheby's catalogue
of May 2002.

with a designated curator, exhibits arranged in a decent order, with proper times when the public can come and ogle. There are also many others that at the moment are basically trophy rooms, which can be seen on special days by special guests.

Five of the public museums are club museums – at Arsenal, Manchester United, Liverpool, West Ham and Celtic. It's expected that five other clubs will have their own museums soon: Aston Villa, Everton, Newcastle, Chelsea and Spurs.

Club museums appeal mostly to fans of their respective clubs, but this should not put off other supporters. They are all part of the same history of football, sharing the same heritage, with very much the same sort of artefacts and displays.

Arsenal's museum opened in 1993 and boasts the biggest collection of a single club's memorabilia in Britain. It tells the story of the club's foundation in 1886 when a group of munition workers got their pennies together to buy a football and start a team. You can see the shirt Alex James wore in the 1936 FA Cup Final, Charlie George's golden boot from the 1971 Final and the big red bus in which Arsenal's winning teams have paraded round Islington – an event, alas for all Spurs fans, which could be happening even more regularly.

Manchester United's museum is bigger, newer, flasher, more expensive, as you might well expect. It attracts 200,000 people a year, which at £8.50 a time for adults, for the museum and a tour, means they can make well over £1 million a year. It tells the club's history from its foundation as Newton Heath by some Lancashire and Yorkshire Railway workers, taking you through the successes and tragedies, such as the Munich air crash. It's very high tech.

Liverpool's museum also opens each day. Pride of place goes to their four European Cups. They are currently working on a plan to recreate their famous Boot Room. Let's hope they can include the smell. West Ham's new museum opened in October 2002 at a cost of £4 million and boasts the personal collections of Bobby Moore, Geoff Hurst and Martin Peters.

Celtic's museum, amongst other excitements, has a 1903 jersey – historic stuff, as that was the first time they wore green hoops. Rangers, as yet, have no separate museum, just a stadium tour and a chance to look at their trophy room.

The Scottish Football Museum is in the newly developed Hampden Park, though their collection has been displayed elsewhere for some years. They

MESTALLA

GRAN PARTIDO DE FUTBOL AMISTOSO

LUNES 15 - ABRIL - 1929

VALENCIA F. C.

CONTRA

SELECCION DE LA ESCUADRA INGLESA

are strong on old shirts and boots. English as well as Scottish football fans, and fans worldwide, will find it of interest as Scotland played such a vital part in the developement of football.

All English fans, regardless of what team they support, should visit the National Museum at Preston which opened in 2001. It's under the stand in the newly developed Deepdale, home of Preston North End. They have 1,000 items on show, such as the world's oldest international shirt, worn by Arnold Kirke Smith while playing for England against Scotland in 1872, and another 20,000 objects behind the scenes, available for researchers. It includes their 1580 copy of the *Calcio*, the world's oldest known football book.

They have nicely combined the educational side, putting football in a social context, showing Dick Kerr's women's team against suffragette images, with lots of fun stuff and interactive games and displays. They have had visits from football officials in Brazil, Germany and Norway and each of these countries is planning now its own version. No foreign country has its own national football museum so far, but Barcelona has its club museum, which is the most visited in the world. At Preston, they had hoped for 80,000 visitors a year but so far have only managed 40,000 a year. It's a brilliant exhibition, beautifully set out, and collecting football memorabilia is now so popular, so why is not attracting more people?

Preston could be part of the reason. Football wise, we know its importance, but the town itself is not much of a tourist trap, unlike Barcelona. It cost £15 million to create, but they've been left with little money for advertising and promotion. The main explanation could be the football psyche. David Beckham has not visited it so far, nor any other present-day stars, but Bobby Charlton and most of the 1966 team have been. Today's players tend to think only of today, not where they and football have come from. Football fans are much the same. It takes time and age for them to realise there is a past.

Another present-day growth connected with the arts and the influence of football is the study of football. Few would have believed 30 years ago that you would ever be able to get a degree in football. We've always had

ABOVE My ticket for the 1966 World Cup, kept as a momento and now worth £150 because of the associations not any intrinsic merit. In the past, ordinary football artefacts were often attractive in themselves, such as the standard cheque issued by Spurs in 1929 for gate expenses. Admire the fancy scroll and the pretty vignette.

Professors of the Pitch, Educated Left Feet, Wizards of Dribble, Prince of Players, Kings of White Hart Lane, but now you can hardly move for Doctors of Football. Real ones, not nicknames, with PhDs.

I got a small clue exactly 30 years ago, when writing *The Glory Game*. At the end of it, I included about 40 pages of appendices, all the bits and pieces, odd facts and stuff, I had not been able to work in, plus some question and answers I'd put to the first-team pool, for amusement as much as anything. Things like pre-match rituals, how they voted, did they help in the house, newspapers read, plans for the future.

For the next ten years or so, almost all the letters I got were not about the book itself but about the appendices, kids doing essays, wanting to include some of my material. Then it moved on to students, till eventually, much to my surprise, folks were getting degrees for studying football.

And why not. It's a huge industry and the history of football is an integral part of our social and cultural life. There are now 50 universities where you can study football, though admittedly in many of them football is just part of sports studies. There are also at least five places where you can do a PhD in football - at De Montfort, Leicester, Birkbeck, Liverpool and Central Lancs.

De Montfort likes to think it's the world's leading centre for football history, thanks to its International Centre for Sports History and Culture, set up in 1996. They have connections with FIFA and get lots of overseas students doing MAs, plus 20 currently doing a PhD. Recent fields of research for PhDs have included women's football, marketing in professional football clubs, the history of the Football League up to 1939. Oh, if only I'd held on and done *The Glory Game* as a thesis not a book. I could have been a PhD by now, if not a Professor.

One of the professors at De Montfort is Tony Mason, author of a very good book about Association Football and English Society (now alas out of print). Along with James Walvin of York, he was one of the first academics to research and write about football history. Back in the 1970s, Tony Mason was dragging football into his lectures at Warwick University. 'But it was made clear to me it was not really an appropriate subject.'

Now, presumably, he must be well chuffed, seeing what strides football has made, the game itself, as well as the study of its history. 'I'm not so sure,' he said. 'I'm beginning to think football is getting too big for its boots ...' Well, that was a surprise. But then in football, Brian, there are always surprises.

Today

19

OUR FOOTBALL has never been more popular, healthier and wealthier, so we all tell ourselves. All regular Premiership players are millionaires, something which seemed unimaginable just ten years ago. Manchester United is the richest club in the world. In 2003, all Premiership games were almost always sold out, with waiting lists for season tickets at the leading clubs. The Premiership, by paying so much in wages and transfers, can afford to bring in the best players from the whole world, so, ergo, we have the world's best league. TV companies at home and channels round the world compete to show our games live. Yes, we are the greatest, we're on a roll.

We have told ourselves such tales before, believed myths we've made up. In the 1950s, we were totally convinced that English football was superior to any other known variety, till Hungary came along. But it is true, English football has been thriving these last ten years, compared with just 20 years ago, in the mid-1980s, when football seemed at rock bottom and gates had dropped by more than half since the immediate post-war years.

There is no argument about the money floating around, especially into the players' pockets. Clubs have to report their total wage bills and in many clubs they were paying out more than they were taking in, which was clearly madness, banking on more money coming in later, so they hoped, when they were doing better, so they hoped.

Top players, like Beckham, Michael Owen and Roy Keane were reported to be earning around £100,000 a week from football in 2003. Beckham's football salary was dwarfed by his commercial income from non-football sources, thanks to advertising and marketing deals with companies like Adidas, Brylcream, Marks and Spencer, Sony and others who were each said to be paying him up to £1 million a year for his name. Altogether, it

OPPOSITE Brazilian hands lifting the World Cup in 2002. It was their fifth success. Will England ever win it again?

was estimated that in 2003, Beckham's total income from all sources was around £10 million.

Manchester United, employer of Beckham and Keane in 2003, was regularly described as the richest club in the world, not because of its gates, as several clubs in Europe, such as Barcelona, got bigger crowds, but its enormous marketing and merchandising income. By 2003, their overall turnover was approaching £200 million a year. Barcelona and Real Madrid were paying more for their players, in wages and transfers, but they were running at a loss, while Manchester United made a profit.

Where would it all end, we all muttered, but people in football, either watching or running it, had been saying similar things for 100 years, ever since Alf Common was sold for £1,000 in 1905. But in 2003, it did look as if more clubs would go bust, unable to pay the high wages when the TV income on which they had depended began to fall after the collapse of ITV Digital in 2002. Several clubs outside the Premiership did declare themselves insolvent, unable to pay wages for a time. Some 300 professional players found themselves out of work, unable to find a club to hire them.

Financially, it did look in 2003 as if the dafter days of money madness were over. Transfer prices had dropped. Clubs would have to stick some sort of cap on wages – if not setting individual limits, as in the old days with a maximum wage, but a communal limit, making sure that the total wage bill did not go above, say, 50 per cent of the club's total income.

Football-wise, the success of the Premiership did rather disguise or distract us from the fact that England's standing in the world rankings was at a modest level, hovering around 10th in the world pecking order, which was not surprising when you look at the facts. England has had only one World Cup win, while Brazil has won it five times, Italy four, Germany three, Argentina and Uruguay twice each. Not once have we won the European Championship.

Even with the Premiership filled now with so many foreign players, if the standard of football has been so brilliant, why between 1992 and 2002 had only one English club won the European Champions League? That was Manchester United in 1999 when they were rather fortunate, coming from behind when all seemed lost. Most experts agree that the Spanish league was stronger – while the top Italian clubs were coming back to form.

But oh, the excitement of the English game, surely that was better than it had ever been? Hard to gauge, impossible to prove, because old teams from

the 1960s will never be able to play their present-day counterparts, except on video games. Football has got faster, that can clearly be seen, and so it should with all the extra emphasis on diet and health and physical preparation.

Players have got bigger and taller, as has the population generally. It's interesting to look at the heights of the Arsenal team today. Almost all are over 6ft tall – Seaman is 6ft 4ins, Campbell 6ft 1in, Cygan 6ft 5ins, Edu 6ft 1in, Pires 6ft 1in, Vieira 6ft 4ins, Bergkamp 6ft, Henry 6ft 2ins, Kanu 6ft 5ins. Freddie Ljungberg, who often appears dwarfed by them all, is in fact 5ft 11ins. In the 1930s, when Arsenal had an equally successful team, only one player at most was ever over six feet. The weights are much the same though, which suggest they were stockier, tougher, in the past, depending more on brawn. They play in ballet shoes today, by comparison with the old days, and many players are now built more like dancers than bruisers. The rules of the game have encouraged more speed and agility. Tackles from behind have gone, back passes to the goalkeeper are not allowed, so the game flows much more freely with fewer interruptions. You have to be fit, just to take part. On the other hand, it seems to me that we are getting

RIGHT Hunter Davies at Highbury in 2003, just to show he spreads his favours around, waiting to see a big team play. Arsenal will soon be leaving Highbury, and their famous East Stand, a listed building, for a new stadium.

more injuries today, perhaps because of the lightweight boots, the speed of the game. It's hard to assemble facts, comparing the number of injuries with pre-war or post-war games, but I reckon that 10 per cent of any team at any time is injured, more than I remember from the 1960s. No team ever seems able to take the field with its best possible eleven. And yet, in these days of large squads, they should be rested more, protecting them from injuries.

Is the football better? I looked at a video of the 1966 World Cup Final the other day and although I was there at the time, I was surprised by the quality of the passing and control, the moves and tactics. I had led myself to believe that football had got cleverer, more organised, more skilful since then.

In normal Premiership games, with all the top-class foreign players, I would say it is on the whole better. The ball can still get given away cheaply, usually due to hurrying, but you rarely get players missing the ball, falling over, slicing it into the crowd. Goalkeepers get vilified of course when they make a simple mistake, but this is mainly because it so rarely happens.

The speed and excitement, the helter-skelter pace of the Premiership, with all teams always going full out, is what appeals to foreign audiences, so we are told, compared with games in Italy where tactics and patience can so often result in stalemate.

Final evidence of the present-day quality of football comes from the fans and the sell-out crowds. In 2003 the Premiership's average gate was 35,000, the highest in the world. (Germany had 33,000, Spain 29,000 and Italy 25,000.)

The FA and the Football League feared at one time that live radio and then television commentaries on football would ruin gates, with people not bothering to turn up. They gave in very slowly, and to their surprise, it has made no difference. So far.

Our English teams are no longer English, with foreign mercenaries just passing through, who know nothing and care less about their club's history, yet still we turn up and shout and cheer. Replica shirts are a rip off, yet fans still buy them, wearing them with pride as they sit in their massed ranks at every ground, like 10,000 expectant, hopeful, often overweight subs, waiting to come on. When Manchester United, Arsenal, Liverpool, Newcastle, Chelsea play in Europe, at awkward places, on awkward midweek days and times, there are always large huddles of their fans, shouting their heads off, waving at the cameras, baring their naked stomachs.

The devotion of the football fan continually amazes, despite all the obstacles put in their way, all the other rival distractions. They should be given the shirts for free, while the players are made to pay for the privilege.

But will they be so potty about football for ever, so craven in putting up with so much? That's what clubs assume, what they are banking on, while doing so little to please and accommodate the fans, apart from taking money off them. Football did almost collapse during the 1970s and 1980s, when gates dropped from a height of 41 million to 16 million. It could happen again. Fans can be pushed only so far. There could be a time when many decide the product isn't worth the money or the effort …

FALSE PROFITS OF DOOM

Predictions about the end of football have always been wrong in the past. Experts were saying in 1900 that the game was finished, professionalism had ruined it. In 1934, Frank Johnston, sports editor of *The Leader*, in his book *The Football Encyclopaedia*, was writing that the quality of football was now so good he couldn't see it getting better. 'Today football has reached its zenith as far as science on the field is concerned and it is difficult to imagine how methods either of attack or defence can be improved.' Stick around. There will be further changes, more developments to come. There always have been. There always will.

And yet despite all the changes, a football fan of the 1950s or even the 1900s could turn up at a game today and understand what was going on. It's still 11 men trying to get a ball into a goal. The moves, the flow up and down the field, some good passing or individual moments of trickery, culminating in a shot on goal, are still appreciated.

The more we know about football's past, the more we see things recurring. Refs have been booed and thought useless since they first arrived. The football authorities have been either autocratic or out of touch since they were first formed. All football clubs have always been seen as greedy and motivated by self-interest.

In 1905, William Pickford, later president of the FA, made some predictions about football 50 years into the future. Although flying was still mainly a fantasy, with Orville and Wright having only managed a short hop, he predicted crowded 'air motors' taking spectators to the ground, the referee controlling play from a hover plane and a loudspeaker broadcasting his decisions, the pitch would be made of rubber, and in a mighty stadium, capable of holding 500,000 for the Cup Final, he saw 'tiers upon tiers of magnificent polished oak and mahogany seats splendidly upholstered and fitted with every convenience, like stage boxes of a West End theatre.' Well, that last bit has come true, more or less. Rubber pitches have been tried – and failed.

In 1956 a writer in the *Big Book of Football Champions* was more modest in his predictions, trying to look only ten years ahead. He saw the maximum wage being abolished and players having freedom to move once out of contract, both of which have happened. He saw a winter break of six weeks in January and February, which still gets discussed. He predicted a British Super League of 18 teams – suggesting it should start with Arsenal, Chelsea and Spurs from London; Portsmouth from the South; Manchester United, Manchester City and Blackpool from Lancashire; Wolves, Birmingham and West Brom from the Midlands; Newcastle United and Sunderland from the North-East; Rangers, Celtic, Hearts, Hibs and Aberdeen from Scotland. His choice is interesting, reflecting the dominant clubs of the 1950s, the ones assumed would be at the top for many years, if not for ever. Today, up to half would be lucky to be classed as elite clubs. But the idea of a British league, including Celtic and Rangers, is regularly touted.

Pendulums do swing, which is reassuring. For almost the last 50 years, Portsmouth has not been considered among the first or second ranks, but is now returning. Liverpool was not mentioned in that 1950's list, and yet it went on to totally dominate the 1980s, as if it would stay there for ever.

I'm not predicting anything, apart from saying that Manchester United in ten years time will not be the dominant club it has been for the last ten years. But I think England in ten years will have become the dominant country in world football. OK, make that Europe. All right, let's say 20 years. Surely, the tide must flow England's way again. All this money, all this interest and investment in football, must surely pay dividends.

I don't think a winter break will ever come. Two referees are possible. I hope the FA doesn't start splitting or diminishing, with the Premier League trying to get even more money and power, but I can see more problems ahead. If football were starting now from scratch, no one would create a system with three ruling bodies – the FA, Football League and Premier League. To have a fourth authority would be madness.

The game will still be here in 100 years time. I have no fear of that. And I think today's spectators, if they all came back, would still be able to understand and enjoy it. After all, it is a very simple game.

APPENDICES
Appendix A: Football Books

A selection of those used and enjoyed while writing this book.
★ = Highly recommended, worth reading, worth owning.

ENCYCLOPAEDIAS, HISTORIES, REFERENCE BOOKS

- ★ed. COX, RUSSELL, Vamplew; *Encyclopaedia of British Football* (Frank Cass 2002). Over 250 entries by experts, mainly academic. Few illustrations but strong on words.
- GOLESWORTHY, Maurice; *Encyclopaedia of Association Football* (Robert Hale 1956).
- ed. BARNET, Norman; *Purnell's New Encyclopaedia of British Football* (1975)
- SOAR, Phil; *Illustrated Encyclopaedia of British Football* (Marshall Cavendish 1971)
- *Sunday Times Illustrated History of Football* (Hamlyn 1994)
- ed. BARRETT, Norman; *Daily Telegraph Football Chronicle* (Carlton Books 1994)
- RADNEDGE, Keir; *Complete Encyclopaedia of Football* (Carlton 1998)
- ★FABIAN AND GREEN, *Association Football* (4 volumes, Caxton 1960). Contributions from football experts of the 1950s; good on history, if now very dated.
- GREEN, Geoffrey; *Official History of the FA Cup* (Heinemann, 1949)
- GREEN, Geoffrey; *History of the FA, 1863–1953* (Naldrett Press 1953)
- ed. SUTCLIFFE, Brierley, Howorth; *The Story of the Football League 1888–1938* – official history (Football League, 1938)
- TYLER, Martin; *The Story of Football* (Marshall Cavendish 1979)
- RICE, Jonathan; *Start of Play* (Prion 1998)
- LEDBROOKE AND TURNER; *Soccer from the Press Box* (Nicholas Kaye 1950)
- THOMSON, Gordon; *The Man In Black; A History of the Football Referee* (Prion 1998)
- INGLIS, Simon; *Football Grounds of England and Wales* (Collins Willow 1983)
- ★SEDDON, Peter; *A Football Compendium – Guide to Books, Films and Music of Association Football* (British Library 1999) Purely for the anoraks; 813 pages, contains details of all books ever produced on football.
- ed. ROLLIN, Jack; *Rothman's Book of Football Records* (1998)
- HUGMAN, Barry; *PFA Players' Records 1946–1988* (Queen Anne Press 1998)

ART, PHOTOGRAPHS, MEMORABILIA, WRITING, COLLECTING

- ★*FIFA Museum Collection* (Edition Q, Berlin 1996). Beautifully produced in three languages. The collection has now moved to the National Football Museum at Preston.
- ★*Football – I Domini del Calcio* (Artificio, Firenze 1990). Also beautifully produced, in Italian, a work of art about the art of football.
- ★ Football – Hulton Getty Picture Collection. Historic snaps of football action through the decades.
- ★TENNANT, John; *Football – The Golden Age* (Cassell Illustrated 2001). Classy photographs but no words.
- HORNBY, Hugh and the National Football Museum; *Football* (Dorling Kindersley 2002)
- McELROY AND MacDOUGALL, *Football Memorabilia* (Carlton 1999)
- SHIEL, Norman; Final Tie: *Cup Finals 1920–39* (Tempus 1999)
- CHESHIRE, Scott; *Chelsea FC Chronicle; Collected Programmes 1907–8* facsimile edition (2002)
- HUNTINGTON-WHITELEY, James; *The Footballer's Year* (art exhibition book 2002)
- ed. HAMILTON, Ian; *Faber Book of Soccer* (Faber 1992)
- DELANEY, Terence; *A Century of Soccer* (Heinemann 1963)
- Ed. TICHER, Mike; *Foul – Best of 1972–76* (Simon and Schuster 1987)
- LITSTER, John; *The Football Programme; A History and Guide* (Tempus 2000)
- BUDD, Graham; *Soccer Memorabilia* (Philip Wilson 2000)
- *Cigarette Card Values*, Murray's Guide (1988)
- THOMPSON, David; *Half-Time; Football and Cigarette Cards 1890–1940* (Murray Cards 1987)

OLD BOOKS – PRE-FIRST WORLD WAR

- ★GIBSON AND PICKFORD, *Association Football and the Men Who Made It* – 4 volumes (Caxton 1904). Each book over 200 pages; so handsome, what every football collector wants. Expect to pay at least £500 in 2003. Also available in facsimile edition from the Association of Football Statisticians.
- *Book of Football* (Amalgamated Press 1906, repro edition Desert Island Books 1997). Excellent history of the game by experts and participants of the time.

- *ALCOCK AND HILL, *Famous Footballers 1895–96* (News of the World 1897). Stunning portraits, some choice captions.
- *ALCOCK, C.W.; *Association Football* (G Bell 1906). Short study, but by one of the founding fathers of the era.
- *JACKSON, N.L.; *Association Football* (G Newnes 1899). By 'Pa' Jackson, founder of The Corinthians.
- SHEARMAN, Montague; *Football* (Badminton Library 1899)
- JONES, J.L.; *Association Football* (Arthur Pearson 1904)
- *Cassells Book of Sports and Pastimes* (1892)
- *Baily's Magazine of Sports and Pastimes* – collected volume (1893)
- ed. EARL OF SUFFOLK; *Encyclopaedia of Sport* – two volumes (Lawrence and Bullen 1897)
- *CB Fry's Magazine* – collected volume (1904–5)
- ed. CORBETT, B.; *Annals of the Corinthians* (Longman 1906)

1920s AND 1930s

- *CATTON, J.A.H.; *Wickets and Goals* (Chapman and Hall 1926). Only half on football, but all of it amusing and informative.
- ed. MACKENZIE, D.; *The Cup* (Period Publications 1932)
- CREEK, F.N.S.; *Association Football* (Dent 1937)
- JOHNSON, F. (of *The Leader*); *Football Encyclopaedia* (Associated Press 1934)
- ed. JOHNSON, F.; *Football Who's Who* (Associated Press 1935)
- *Encyclopaedia of Sports and Pastimes* (Fleetway House 1935)

SOCIAL HISTORY, ACADEMIC

- *WALVIN, James; *The People's Game* (Mainstream 1994). Academic, but easy to read by a one-time Professor of History at York University.
- WALVIN, James; *The Only Game* (Longman 2001)
- HUTCHINSON, John; *The Football Industry* (Richard Drew 1982)
- MASON, Tony; *Association Football and English Society, 1863–1915* (Harvester Press 1980).
- RUSSELL, Dave; *Football and the English: Social History 1863–1995* (Carnegie 1997)
- GIULIANOTTI, Richard; *Football: A Sociology of the Global Game* (Polity Press 1999)

WOMEN FOOTBALLERS

- NEWSHAM, Gail; *In A League Of Their Own* (Scarlet Press 1997)

BLACK FOOTBALLERS

- VASILI, Phil; *The First Black Footballer – Arthur Wharton* (London 1998)
- VASILI, Phil; *Colouring Over The White Line* (Mainstream 2000)

INDIVIDUAL CLUBS/TOWNS

- ed. CLARKE, James; *History of Football in Kendal 1871–1908* (Kendal 1908)
- WALLACE, Keith; *Barbarians of Workington: history of Uppies and Downies* – two volumes (Castle Curios 1991 and 1997)
- *Celtic: Football Legends 1888–1938* (Stuart Marshall 1998)
- SOAR, Phil and Tyler, Martin; *Official Illustrated History of Arsenal 1886–2000* (Hamlyn 2000)
- *Official Manchester United Illustrated Encyclopaedia* (Andre Deutsch 1998)
- WAGSTAFFE SIMMONS, G.; *History of Tottenham Hotspur 1882–1946* (THFC 1947)

BIOGRAPHIES

Far, far too many, so two old and two new;

- JACK, David; *Soccer* (Unwin 1934)
- SHACKLETON, Len; *Clown Prince of Soccer* (Nicholas Kaye 1955)
- FERGUSON, Alex; *Managing My Life* (Hodder 1999)
- KEANE, Roy; *My Life* (Penguin 2002)

OLD NEWSPAPERS AND MAGAZINES

- *Sporting Chronicle* issues from July-December 1888
- *Cricket and Football Field* 1886
- *Boys Herald* 1906
- *Boys Own* 1913
- *Football Favourite* issues from 1921
- *Pilot Better Football* 1935
- *Topical Times* issues from 1930s
- *Football Digest* 1973
- *Football League Reviews* 1960s–70s.
- *Charles Buchan's Football Monthly* 1950s–70s

FOOTBALL ANNUALS

- *Morning Leader* 1911–12
- *Echo Football Guide*, Darlington, issues 1914–1930s
- *Handy Football Guide* 1924–5
- *Athletic News* issues from 1918–39
- *Daily News* 1921–39
- *Topical Times* issues from 1920s–40s
- *All Sports* 1922–6
- *News Chronicle* 1932
- *The Leader* 1930s
- *Empire News Football Annual* 1930s–50s
- *Post Annual*, Nottingham 1930s–50s
- *Littlewood's* 1935–36
- *Rothman's Football Annuals* 1970–1, 2002–3
- *News of the World* 2002–3

Appendix B: Winners

FOOTBALL LEAGUE WINNERS, FIRST DIVISION FROM 1888 AND PREMIER LEAGUE FROM 1992

FOOTBALL LEAGUE

1888–89 Preston North End
1889–90 Preston North End
1890–1 Everton

OLD FIRST DIVISION

1891–2 Sunderland
1892–3 Sunderland
1893–4 Aston Villa
1894–5 Sunderland
1895–6 Aston Villa
1896–7 Aston Villa
1897–8 Sheffield United
1898–9 Aston Villa
1899–1900 Aston Villa
1900–1 Liverpool
1901–2 Sunderland
1902–3 The Wednesday
1903–4 The Wednesday
1904–5 Newcastle United
1905–6 Liverpool
1906–7 Newcastle United
1907–8 Manchester United
1908–9 Newcastle United
1909–10 Aston Villa

1910–11 Manchester United
1911–12 Blackburn Rovers
1912–13 Sunderland
1913–14 Blackburn Rovers
1914–15 Everton
1919–20 W.B.A
1920–1 Burnley
1921–2 Liverpool
1922–3 Liverpool
1923–4 Huddersfield Town
1924–5 Huddersfield Town
1925–6 Huddersfield Town
1926–7 Newcastle United
1927–8 Everton
1928–9 Sheffield Wednesday
1929–30 Sheffield Wednesday
1930–1 Arsenal
1931–2 Everton
1932–3 Arsenal
1933–4 Arsenal
1934–5 Arsenal
1935–6 Sunderland
1936–7 Manchester City
1937–8 Arsenal

1938–9 Everton
1946–7 Liverpool
1947–8 Arsenal
1948–9 Portsmouth
1949–50 Portsmouth
1950–1 Tottenham
1951–2 Manchester United
1952–3 Arsenal
1953–4 Wolves
1954–5 Chelsea
1955–6 Manchester United
1956–7 Manchester United
1957–8 Wolves
1958–9 Wolves
1959–60 Burnley
1960–1 Tottenham
1961–2 Ipswich Town
1962–3 Everton
1963–4 Liverpool
1964–5 Manchester United
1965–6 Liverpool
1966–7 Manchester United
1967–8 Manchester City
1968–9 Leeds United
1969–70 Everton
1970–1 Arsenal
1971–2 Derby County
1972–3 Liverpool
1973–4 Leeds United

1974–5 Derby County
1975–6 Liverpool
1976–7 Liverpool
1977–8 Nottingham Forest
1978–9 Liverpool
1979–80 Liverpool
1980–1 Aston Villa
1981–2 Liverpool
1982–3 Liverpool
1983–4 Liverpool
1984–5 Everton
1985–6 Liverpool
1986–7 Everton
1987–8 Liverpool
1988–9 Arsenal
1989–90 Liverpool
1990–1 Arsenal
1991–2 Leeds United

F.A PREMIER LEAGUE

1992–3 Manchester United
1993–4 Manchester United
1994–5 Blackburn Rovers
1995–6 Manchester United
1996–7 Manchester United
1997–8 Arsenal
1998–9 Manchester United
1999–2000 Manchester United
2000–01 Manchester United
2001–02 Arsenal

FA CUP WINNERS SINCE 1872

At Kennington Oval
1872 The Wanderers beat Royal Engineers 1-0

At Lillie Bridge, London
1873 The Wanderers beat Oxford University 2-1

At Kennington Oval
1874 Oxford University beat Royal Engineers 2-0
1875 Royal Engineers beat Old Etonians 2-0 after a 1-1 draw
1876 The Wanderers beat Old Etonians 3-0 after a 0-0 draw
1877 The Wanderers beat Oxford University 2-1
1878 The Wanderers beat Royal Engineers 3-1
1879 Old Etonians beat Clapham Rovers 1-0
1880 Clapham Rovers beat Oxford University 1-0
1881 Old Carthusians beat Old Etonians 3-0
1882 Old Etonians beat Blackburn Rovers 1-0
1883 Blackburn Olympic beat Old Etonians 2-1
1884 Blackburn Rovers beat Queen's Park (Glasgow) 2-1
1885 Blackburn Rovers beat Queen's Park (Glasgow) 2-0
1886 Blackburn Rovers beat West Bromwich Albion 2-0
      after a 0-0 draw
1887 Aston Villa beat West Bromwich Albion 2-0
1888 West Bromwich Albion beat Preston North End 2-1
1889 Preston North End beat Wolves 3-0
1890 Blackburn Rovers beat Sheffield Wednesday 6-1

1891 Blackburn Rovers beat Notts County 3-1
1892 West Bromwich Albion beat Aston Villa 3-0

At Fallowfield, Manchester
1893 Wolves beat Everton 1-0

At Goodison Park
1894 Notts County beat Bolton Wanderers 4-1

At Crystal Palace
1895 Aston Villa beat West Bromwich Albion 1-0
1896 Sheffield Wednesday beat Wolves 2-1
1897 Aston Villa beat Everton 3-2
1898 Nottingham Forest beat Derby County 3-1
1899 Sheffield United beat Derby County 4-1
1900 Bury beat Southampton 4-0
1901 Tottenham beat Sheffield United 3-1 after a 2-2 draw
1902 Sheffield United beat Southampton 2-1 after a 1-1 draw
1903 Bury beat Derby County 6-0
1904 Manchester City beat Bolton Wanderers
1905 Aston Villa beat Newcastle United 2-0
1906 Everton beat Newcastle United 1-0
1907 Sheffield Wednesday beat Everton 2-1
1908 Wolves beat Newcastle United 3-1
1909 Manchester United beat Bristol City 1-0
1910 Newcastle United beat Barnsley 2-0 after a 1-1 draw
1911 Bradford City beat Newcastle United 1-0 after a 0-0 draw

1912 Barnsley beat West Bromwich Albion 1-0 after a 0-0 draw
1913 Aston Villa beat Sunderland 1-0
1914 Burnley beat Liverpool 1-0

At Old Trafford
1915 Sheffield United beat Chelsea 3-0

At Stamford Bridge
1920 Aston Villa beat Huddersfield Town 1-0
1921 Tottenham beat Wolves 1-0
1922 Huddersfield Town beat Preston North End 1-0

At Wembley
1923 Bolton Wanderers beat West Ham United 2-0
1924 Newcastle United beat Aston Villa 2-0
1925 Sheffield United beat Cardiff City 1-0
1926 Bolton Wanderers beat Manchester City 1-0
1927 Cardiff City beat Arsenal 1-0
1928 Blackburn Rovers beat Huddersfield Town 3-1
1929 Bolton Wanderers beat Portsmouth 2-0
1930 Arsenal beat Huddersfield Town 2-0
1931 West Bromwich Albion beat Birmingham City 2-1
1932 Newcastle United beat Arsenal 2-1
1933 Everton beat Manchester City 3-0
1934 Manchester City beat Portsmouth 2-1
1935 Sheffield Wednesday beat West Bromwich Albion 4-2
1936 Arsenal beat Sheffield United 1-0
1937 Sunderland beat Preston North End 3-1
1938 Preston North End beat Huddersfield Town 1-0
1939 Portsmouth beat Wolves 4-1
1946 Derby County beat Charlton Athletic 4-1
1947 Charlton Athletic beat Burnley 1-0
1948 Manchester United beat Blackpool 4-2
1949 Wolves beat Leicester City 3-1
1950 Arsenal beat Liverpool 2-0
1951 Newcastle United beat Blackpool 2-0
1952 Newcastle United beat Arsenal 1-0
1953 Blackpool beat Bolton Wanderers 4-3
1954 West Bromwich Albion beat Preston North End 3-2
1955 Newcastle United beat Manchester City 3-1
1956 Manchester City beat Birmingham City 3-1
1957 Aston Villa beat Manchester United 2-1
1958 Bolton Wanderers beat Manchester United 2-0
1959 Nottingham Forest beat Luton Town 2-1
1960 Wolves beat Blackburn Rovers 3-0
1961 Tottenham beat Leicester City 2-0
1962 Tottenham beat Burnley 3-1
1963 Manchester United beat Leicester City 3-1
1964 West Ham United beat Preston North End 3-2
1965 Liverpool beat Leeds United 2-1
1966 Everton beat Sheffield Wednesday 3-2
1967 Tottenham beat Chelsea 2-1
1968 West Bromwich Albion beat Everton 1-0
1969 Manchester City beat Leicester City 1-0
1970 Chelsea beat Leeds United 2-1 after a 2-2 draw
1971 Arsenal beat Liverpool 2-1

1972 Leeds United beat Arsenal 1-0
1973 Sunderland beat Leeds United 1-0
1974 Liverpool beat Newcastle United 3-0
1975 West Ham United beat Fulham 2-0
1976 Southampton beat Manchester United 1-0
1977 Manchester United beat Liverpool 2-1
1978 Ipswich Town beat Arsenal 1-0
1979 Arsenal beat Manchester United 3-2
1980 West Ham United beat Arsenal 1-0
1981 Tottenham beat Manchester City 3-2 after a 1-1 draw
1982 Tottenham beat Queen's Park Rangers 1-0 after a 1-1 draw
1983 Manchester United beat Brighton and Hove Albion 4-0 after a 2-2 draw
1984 Everton beat Watford 2-0
1985 Manchester United beat Everton 1-0
1986 Liverpool beat Everton 3-1
1987 Coventry City beat Tottenham 3-2
1988 Wimbledon beat Liverpool 1-0
1989 Liverpool beat Everton 3-2
1990 Manchester United beat Crystal Palace 1-0 after a 3-3 draw
1991 Tottenham beat Nottingham Forest 2-1
1992 Liverpool beat Sunderland 2-0
1993 Arsenal beat Sheffield Wednesday 2-1 after a 1-1 draw
1994 Manchester United beat Chelsea 4-0
1995 Everton beat Manchester United 1-0
1996 Manchester United beat Liverpool 1-0
1997 Chelsea beat Middlesbrough 2-0
1998 Arsenal beat Newcastle United 2-0
1999 Manchester United beat Newcastle United 2-0
2000 Chelsea beat Aston Villa 1-0

At Millennium Stadium
2001 Liverpool beat Arsenal 2-1
2002 Arsenal beat Chelsea 2-0

WORLD CUP WINNERS SINCE 1930

Year	Winners	Score	Runners-up	Score	Venue	Attendance
1930	Uruguay	4	Argentina	2	Montevideo	90,000
1934	Italy	2	Czechoslovakia	1	Rome	50,000
1938	Italy	4	Hungary	2	Paris	45,000
1950	Uruguay	2	Brazil	1	Rio de Janeiro	199,854
1954	West Germany	3	Hungary	2	Berne	60,000
1958	Brazil	5	Sweden	2	Stockholm	49,737
1962	Brazil	3	Czechoslovakia	1	Santiago	68,679
1966	England	4	West Germany	2	Wembley	93,802
1970	Brazil	4	Italy	1	Mexico City	107,412
1974	West Germany	2	Holland	1	Munich	77,833
1978	Argentina	3	Holland	1	Buenos Aires	77,000
1982	Italy	3	West Germany	1	Madrid	90,080
1986	Argentina	3	West Germany	2	Mexico City	114,580
1990	West Germany	1	Argentina	0	Rome	73,603
1994	Brazil	0	Italy	0	Los Angeles	94,194
1998	France	3	Brazil	0	St Denis	75,000
2002	Brazil	2	Germany	0	Yokohama	69,029

INDEX

PICTURE CREDITS

The publisher has made every effort to clear permissions for the illustrative material in this book and apologises for any inadvertent omissions that have been made.

pages 1, 2, 7, 13, 16, 21, 24, 29, 30, 33, 34, 38, 40, 41, 44, 47, 48, 49, 50, 51, 52r, 53, 58, 61, 62, 66, 68, 73, 74, 77, 81, 84, 93, 95, 96, 97, 99, 100, 101, 102, 105, 106, 107, 108, 109, 110, 113, 115, 116, 118, 119, 120-121, 135, 163, 171, 180, 202, 210, 212, 218, 229, 230, 231, 233, 235, 236 courtesy of Hunter Davies:
pages 18, 22-23, 37, 52, 56, 65, 208, 213, 228 National Football Museum
pages 78 Popperfoto; 169 R. Saidman/Popperfoto; 219 Peter Waugh/Popperfoto
pages 90, 124-125 H. F. Davies/Hulton; 155 Jamie McDonald Getty Images; 175, 179 bottom right, 201 top, 203, 238 Getty Images; 178 David Cannon/Getty Images; 183 Shaun Botterill/Getty Images; 215 Edward G. Malindine/Hulton; 241 Laurence Griffiths/Getty Images; 148 Leonard Burt/Hulton; 14-15, 42, 54-55, 70-71, 80, 81, 82, 83, 86-87, 89, 122, 126, 144-145, 150 Hulton
pages 129 Barratts/ALPHA/Empics; 130, 136, 147, 174 right, 200 Empics; 170 Matthew Ashton/Empics; 156 Mike Egerton/Empics; 157, 160, 192, 195 Peter Robinson/Empics; 180 Paul Marriot/Empics; 196, 206 Tony Marshall/Empics; 166, 181, 194, 204 S&G/ALPHA/Empics; 167, 177, 179 top left Neal Simpson/Empics
page 132 Littlewoods Pools
pages 140, 149, 152, 164 Topham Picturepoint; 151 Star Images/Topham Picturepoint; 159, 179 centre left Universal Pictorial Press Ltd., London/Topham Picturepoint; 168 PAL/Topham Picturepiont; 179 centre right Press Association/Owen Humphreys/Topham Picturepoint
page 172 Corbis U.K. Ltd
pages 221, 232 The Ronald Grant Archive
page 223 Alan Cristea Gallery/*F is for Football*, from *The Alphabet*, 1991, © Peter Blake 2003. All rights reserved DACS
pages 226-227 courtesy of Alfred Daniels
pages 242, 244-245 Stuart Clarke (www.homesoffootball.co.uk)